Beginner Rock
Guitar Lessons

Book & Videos   Damon Ferrante

Guitar Instruction Guide to Learn How to Play Licks, Chords, Scales, Techniques, Lead & Rhythm Guitar, Basic Music Theory, and Exercises - Teach Yourself or Work with an Instructor (Book, Videos & TAB)

HOW THE BOOK & VIDEOS WORK

The idea for this book grew out of my experiences teaching beginner guitar students Rock styles over the last twenty-five years. I was looking for a book that would be inspiring and exciting for beginner Rock guitarists--helping them learn licks, riffs, techniques and basic music theory. Even though there are a number of guitar books available for beginners, they all seem to promote a monotonous, creativity-sapping approach where beginner Rock guitarists aimlessly repeat the same dull exercises over and over, often practicing things that they would never use in real songs or in live performance situations.

Since, after searching the music book landscape for years, I could not find a beginner Rock guitar book that would help guitarists develop and improve their playing in a fun and engaging manner, I decided to work with Steeplechase Arts to write one myself. The approach that this book and video course takes is to consider each reader, regardless of his or her musical goals, as an artist who has a unique and valid musical voice. The book and videos seek to inspire each beginner Rock guitarist to develop his or her own musical style and personality through a combination of the essential elements of beginner Rock guitar: licks and techniques, chord and rhythm styles, lead guitar, blues styles, an understanding of guitar gear, basic music theory, and thoughts on advancing in your guitar playing.

The book and videos follow a step-by-step lesson format for beginner-level Rock guitar playing. There are 100 lessons in the book and 32 corresponding video lessons. The lessons cover a broad range of subjects, related to beginner-level Rock guitar playing, that will help you become both a better guitarist and a better musician. The lessons not only help you build your technique, expressivity and fluidity, but are also designed to promote your creativity and musicality.

All of the examples in this book are given in tablature ("TAB" for short) and have corresponding video lesson examples. This way, by watching the videos, you can see and hear how to play each technique and music example. There is **no** music reading necessary to work with this book and video course. To make the concepts easier for beginners, the book only uses tablature and chord diagrams for the songs and music examples.

Given that the focus of the book is beginner Rock guitar, a special emphasis is placed on electric guitar playing and techniques. However, most of the material, with the exception of the sections that cover the electric guitar specifically, can also be easily played on an acoustic guitar.

INTRODUCTION: CHAPTER OVERVIEW

Beginner Rock Guitar Lessons is composed of five chapters and 32 corresponding video lessons that cover all of the essential elements for getting started playing Rock guitar. Each lesson builds on the next in a steady, gradual, and progressive manner. You become a better guitarist by going step by step through each chapter, video and lesson of the book.

Chapter 1: Starting Out: This section of the book and videos goes over the parts of the guitar, strumming techniques, easy guitar chords, buying a guitar and amp, tuning the guitar, the names of the strings, and all of the initial concepts that you will need to begin rocking out on guitar. No experience with guitar or music is necessary to work with this book. So, this chapter starts things out at the ground floor.

Chapter 2: Rock Guitar Basics: This section builds on the concepts from the previous one, taking things a little further. The chapter and corresponding videos cover major and minor chords, alternate picking, power chords, slide techniques and licks, tablature (TAB), chord theory, how to change the guitar strings, Rock jam tracks, and music theory on intervals.

Chapter 3: Blues Rock Basics: This section of the book and videos gives you the essential elements to delve deeper into Rock guitar. It covers the Blues scale and licks, Rockabilly grooves, seventh chords, music theory on chord progressions, Blues jam tracks and songs, vibrato technique and licks, and twelve-bar blues.

Chapter 4: Rhythm Guitar: This chapter and its corresponding video lessons bring your musicality to a higher level, now that you have advanced beyond the beginner stages of your guitar playing. It covers palm muting techniques, Funk and Reggae styles, Barre chords, strumming patterns, Blues bass lines, arpeggiated chords, ballad styles, and rhythm-guitar riffs.

Chapter 5: Lead Guitar Basics: By the final section of the book and videos, you have significantly improved your guitar playing. This chapter helps you develop things further and elevates your playing toward an intermediate level. The chapter and videos cover hammer-on and pull-off techniques and licks, an overview of guitar pedals, string-bending techniques and licks, getting different tones from your guitar, double-stop techniques and licks, and ideas on how to craft good guitar solos.

The Video Lessons: There are 32 streaming video lessons that correspond to the lessons in the book. The video lessons cover and demonstrate guitar techniques and licks, music theory, song and jam tracks, and gear overviews. All of the video lessons are **free** and available at SteeplechaseMusic.com. Just go to the Home Page and click the link on the top of the page for Guitar Books. Then, on the Guitar Books webpage, click *Beginner Rock Guitar Lessons.* **No** registration or sign-up is needed to view the video lessons and there is no limit to the amount of times that they may be viewed.

TABLE OF CONTENTS

CHAPTER 4: RHYTHM GUITAR

CHAPTER 5: LEAD GUITAR BASICS

ABOUT THE AUTHOR / APPENDIX

TABLE OF CONTENTS FOR THE VIDEOS

Steeplechase Music Books

Also by Damon Ferrante

Ultimate Guitar Chords, Scales & Arpeggios Handbook: 240-Lesson, Step-By-Step Guitar Guide, Beginner to Advanced Levels (Book & Videos)

Guitar Scales Handbook: A Step-By-Step, 100-Lesson Guide to Scales, Music Theory, and Fretboard Theory (Book & Videos)

Guitar Adventures: A Fun, Informative, and Step-By-Step 60-Lesson Guide to Chords, Beginner & Intermediate Levels, with Companion Lesson and Play-Along Videos

Piano Scales, Chords & Arpeggios Lessons with Elements of Basic Music Theory: Fun, Step-By-Step Guide for Beginner to Advanced Levels (Book & Videos)

Little Piano Book: Fun, Step-By-Step, Easy-To-Follow, 60-Lesson Song and Beginner Piano Guide to Get You Started (Book & Videos)

Guitar Arpeggio Handbook, 2nd Edition: 120-Lesson, Step-By-Step Guide to Guitar Arpeggios, Music Theory, and Technique-Building Exercises, Beginner to Advanced Levels (Book & Videos)

Guitar Adventures for Kids, Level 1: Fun, Step-By-Step, Beginner Lesson Guide to Get You Started (Book & Videos)

Adult Piano Elements Complete Course: Teach Yourself Piano--Fun, Step-By-Step Beginner to Intermediate Piano Song & Lesson Guide (Book & Videos)

Dreaming Cities: A Piano Trio

The Mountain & Tidewater Songs: Song Cycle for Baritone and Piano Trio

Snow Moon: Piano Sonata

GOOD NEWS!

This edition of *Beginner Rock Guitar Lessons* includes free, bonus lessons. Go to the Home Page of SteeplechaseMusic.com. At the top of the Home Page, you will see a link for Guitar Books. Follow the link to the Guitar Books webpage. Then, click on the link for *Beginner Rock Guitar Lessons.*

Have Fun!

Beginner Rock Guitar Lessons: Guitar Instruction Guide to Learn How to Play Licks, Chords, Scales, Techniques, Lead & Rhythm Guitar, Basic Music Theory, and Exercises--Teach Yourself or Work with an Instructor (Book, Videos & TAB)

by Damon Ferrante
Steeplechase Arts & Productions, LLC

ISBN-13: 978-0692335802 (Steeplechase Arts)

ISBN-10: 0692335803

Symbols Used In This Book

1 • 1st Finger (Index Finger)

2 • 2nd Finger (Middle Finger)

3 • 3rd Finger (Ring Finger)

4 • 4th Finger (Pinky Finger)

1 • Place Finger over 2 or more strings.

O • Open String (Let the String Vibrate.)

X • Mute String (Block the String with a Finger.)

Instructional Videos:

- There are 32 Supplemental Instructional Videos that correspond to the lessons in this Book.
- The Videos provide additional instruction and play-along recordings.
- These Videos are <u>Free</u> and Available at <u>SteeplechaseMusic.com</u>
- Go to the Home Page. Click on Guitar Books. Then, click on the cover for this book.
- No Registration is needed to view the Videos and there is no limit to the amount of times they may be viewed.

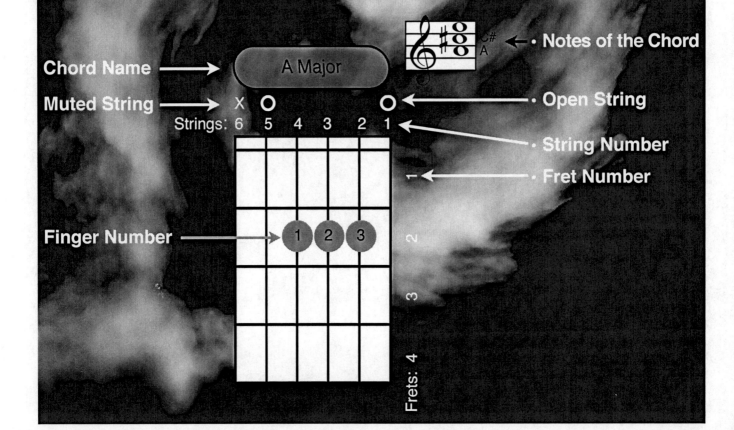

Chord Name → A Major

← • Notes of the Chord

Muted String → X ○ ○ ← • Open String

Strings: 6 5 4 3 2 1 ← • String Number

← • Fret Number

Finger Number → 1 2 3

Frets: 4

CHAPTER ONE: STARTING OUT

Lesson 1:
Secret to Guitar Success #1

Over the course of this book and videos, you will learn new techniques and licks, basic concepts about how music is put together (otherwise known as "music theory"), and an overview of the gear you will need for Rock guitar playing. Interspersed alongside these music concepts are short essays entitled "Secrets to Guitar Success." The idea of these "secrets" is to give you a chance to step back from your playing and take a look at where you are and where you are going, musically speaking. The "secrets" are designed to be starting points for you to think about different aspects of your music making-- from day-to-day matters to long-range plans. They are based on general concepts that I have learned over the years from teachers (both in music and other aspects of life) as well as insights from students. I hope that they might be ideas that you return to from time to time and that they help you in your progress to becoming a better musician.

Secret #1: *Have a Positive Attitude, Enjoy the Process, and Have Fun*

One of the most important aspects for learning an instrument is cultivating a positive attitude. If you approach learning guitar with a happy, fun-loving spirit your mind and body will be much more receptive to learning new ideas. Having a can-do, positive outlook will not only make the process of learning more fun, but it has been proven to speed up the process of improving. So, you should always approach your guitar playing as an exciting and rewarding activity of your day.

If you are feeling tired, a little down, or having a bad day and reluctant to practice your guitar, just remind yourself about how playing the guitar always makes you feel better and gives you positive energy. Sometimes, all it takes is grabbing your guitar, smiling and saying in your head -- "This is Fun!"

Give it a try!

Lesson 2: Types of Guitars

Acoustic
Guitar

Solid-Body
Electric Guitar

Hollow-Body
Electric Guitar

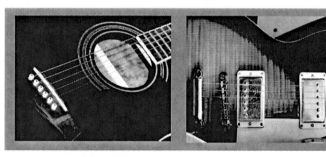

Acoustic Guitar
Sound Hole

Electric Guitar
Pickups

Although there are countless varieties of guitars in the world, ranging from neon-green, polka-dotted models to lightning-shaped ones, most guitars fit into three main, broad categories: Acoustic Guitars (Steel-String and Nylon-String), Solid-Body Electric Guitars, and Hollow-Body Electric Guitars.

Acoustic Guitars have a hollow body that allows for a natural amplification of the sound caused by the vibrating strings. Most Acoustic Guitars fall into two main categories: Steel-String and Nylon-String Guitars. Steel-String Guitars have all metal strings and, generally, have a bright and metallic sound. Nylon-String Guitars, often used for Classical guitar playing, have a combination of metal-wound strings for the low-sounding, bass strings and nylon strings for the thinner, higher-sounding strings.

Solid-Body Electric Guitars are the most common type of electric guitar. In and of themselves, they have a fairly quiet sound, since they do not have a hollow chamber (like acoustic guitars) to enhance the sound. For electric guitars, the sound of the vibrating strings is drawn from the wood of the guitar body through the pickups (a series of wound, magnetic coils) located below the strings in the center of the front of the guitar. (See Lesson 4 for more information). The sound then travels through a cable to an amplifier ("amp" for short).

Hollow-Body Electric Guitars are electric guitars that combine the features of Solid-Body Electric and Acoustic Guitars. They have a fairly resonant sound, in and of themselves, and they can also be amplified.

Lesson 3
Parts of an Acoustic Guitar

Here is an example of a steel-string acoustic guitar. They have a vibrant sound. In general, acoustic guitars have a higher action (the distance between the string and the fretboard). One of the benefits of acoustic guitars is that they are easily portable and don't need an amplifier.

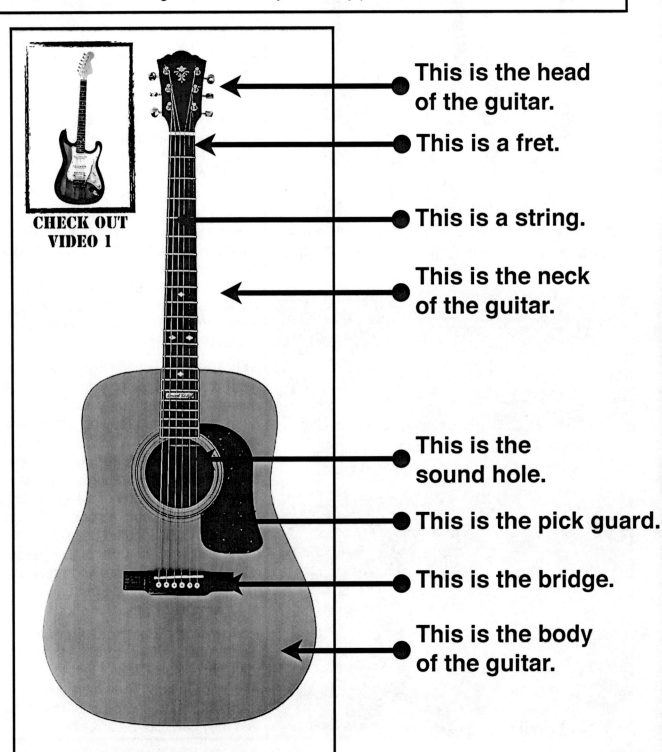

CHECK OUT VIDEO 1

This is the head of the guitar.

This is a fret.

This is a string.

This is the neck of the guitar.

This is the sound hole.

This is the pick guard.

This is the bridge.

This is the body of the guitar.

Lesson 4
Parts of an Electric Guitar

If you have an electric guitar, try to locate each of these parts. Since there is a wide range of design styles for electric guitars, you will probably find a few differences (in some of the details) from the electric guitar example in the illustration below.

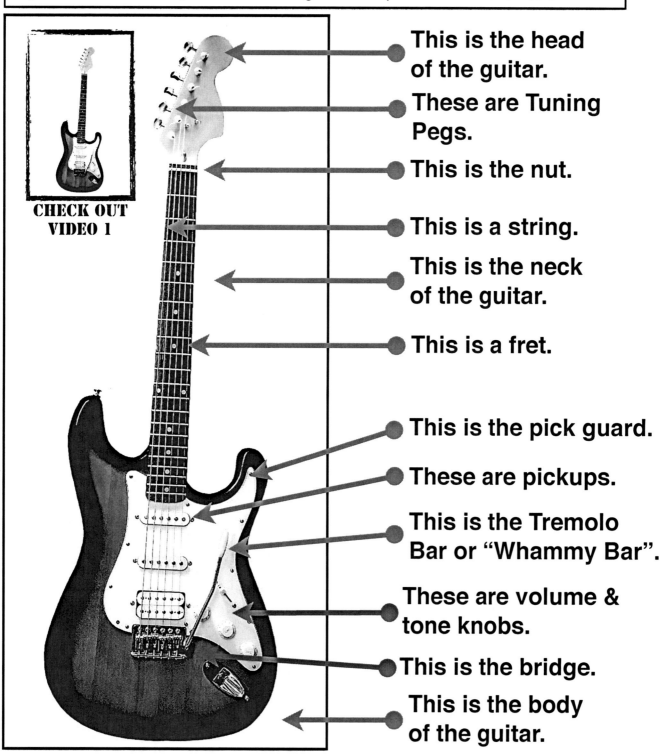

CHECK OUT VIDEO 1

This is the head of the guitar.

These are Tuning Pegs.

This is the nut.

This is a string.

This is the neck of the guitar.

This is a fret.

This is the pick guard.

These are pickups.

This is the Tremolo Bar or "Whammy Bar".

These are volume & tone knobs.

This is the bridge.

This is the body of the guitar.

Lesson 5: An Explanation of the Different Parts of the Guitar

The **Head** of the guitar is the top section of the guitar. It holds the tuning pegs. There is often a company logo on the head of the guitar.

The **Tuning Pegs** (sometimes called "machine heads") are metal or plastic knobs, located on the guitar head. They allow the guitarist to adjust the tension on the strings. By turning a tuning peg and increasing the tension on the string, the sound of that string will have a higher pitch. The opposite is true if you loosen the tension on the string: the sound of the string will be lower.

The **Neck** of the guitar is a long section of wood that connects the head and body of the guitar. The frets and fingerboard are on the top of the neck.

The **Nut** is a small piece of plastic or wood, located between the head and neck. The nut helps keep the strings above the frets and fingerboard.

The **Frets** are rectangular boxes that run up and down the guitar neck. They are created by small strips of metal that cover the guitar neck at precise spacing. These frets create the specific notes on the guitar, for instance, the note "C" or the note "F-Sharp". At the head of the guitar, the frets are wider. As you travel "up" the guitar neck toward the body, the frets become thinner, because the pitches ("sounds") are getting higher.

The **Body** of the guitar is a large, often curved, section of wood. On acoustic guitars it holds the bridge, sound hole, and pick guard. On electric guitars, it is the part of the guitar that holds the pickups, bridge, tone and volume knobs, toggle switch, pick guard, and whammy bar.

The **Pickups** are sets of wound, magnetic coils. They are often housed in plastic or metal casings. The pickups draw the vibrations from the strings and send them through the cable to the amplifier. (We will go into more detail about pickups and amplifiers later in this book. They are an important part of the character of each electric guitar's sound.)

The **Bridge** is a piece of wood or metal that is located on the body of the guitar. The strings are held in tension between the bridge and the tuning pegs of the guitar.

The **Sound Hole** is the circular hole on the body of an acoustic guitar. The sound of the vibrating strings travels through the sound hole in the the body of an acoustic guitar. The sound is then "amplified" by the interior of the guitar body and projected back out of the sound hole.

The **Tremolo Bar** (or "Whammy Bar") is a metal bar attached to the bridge of electric guitars. It allows the guitarist to pull up or push down on the bridge and increase or decrease the tension on the strings: raising or lowing the sound of the notes.

The **Volume** and **Tone** knobs on an electric guitar raise and lower the loudness of the guitar's sound and also change the balance of treble and bass sound for the guitar. On an electric guitar, these knobs can greatly change the sound of the instrument. In some ways these knobs create "many instruments in one". Later on in this book, we are going to go through more details about how you can use the volume and tone knobs in your playing.

Lesson 6: Names of the Guitar Strings & Finger Numbers

In this lesson, we are going to learn two concepts:
The letter names for the guitar strings and the finger numbers for the left hand.

Low
E A D G B **High**
E

The Guitar Strings

- 6th String, **Low E = Ernie**
- 5th String, **A = Always**
- 4th String, **D = Drinks**
- 3rd String, **G = Grape Juice**
- 2nd String, **B = Before**
- 1st String, **High E = Eating**

- The guitar has six strings.
- The strings have numbers that go from the thinnest string to the thickest string.
- The thinnest string is string #1. It is located closest to the floor and it has the highest sound.
- The thickest string is string #6. It is located closest to the ceiling and has the lowest (or deepest) sound.
- The thinnest string (the first string) is called the "High-E String".
- The thickest string (the sixth string) is called the "Low-E String".
- Going from thickest string to thinnest string, here are the letter names for the strings:

Low E, A, D, G, B, High E

- To help you remember the letter names and order for the strings, here is a silly sentence: **E**rnie **A**lways **D**rinks **G**rape Juice **B**efore **E**ating.
- The first letter of each word (**except for "juice"**) stands for a string of the guitar, going from thickest string to thinnest string. **See the chart on the left.**

- Try this exercise: While holding your guitar, try to find the Low-E String and play it. Now, try to find the High-E String and play it.
- Now, go through all of the strings, from Low E to High E, and play them in order (thickest string to thinnest), while saying the letter name for each string.

Left-Hand Finger Numbers:
Index Finger = 1, Middle Finger = 2, Ring Finger = 3, Pinky = 4

Lesson 7: Holding the Pick & Left-Hand Technique

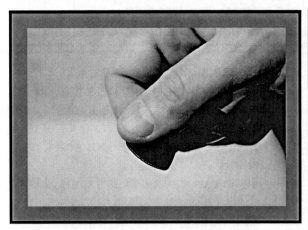

Holding the guitar pick

Try this exercise: Find the 1st string (the High-E String). With a downward motion, pluck the string 10 times in a row. Then, with an upward motion, pluck the string 10 times in a row. Repeat this.

Let's look at how to hold the guitar pick.

- Gently place the guitar pick on the finger nail of your Right-Hand Index Finger.

- It should be resting gently on top of your finger nail.

- Then, slide it to the left side of your Index Finger.

- Finally, gently place your Right-Hand Thumb over over the guitar pick. It should be held between your Right-Hand Thumb and Index Finger. (See the Photo on the left.)

Left-Hand Technique

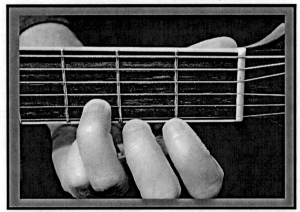

Try this exercise (see the photo above): Place the 3rd finger of your left hand on the 3rd fret of the 2nd string (the B String). Pluck the string with your pick. This is the note "D", by the way. Then, lift your finger off the string and pluck the open string. This is the note "B". Repeat this 10 times in a row.

Let's Look at Basic Left-Hand Technique

- For most of your guitar playing you are going to want to play the guitar notes with the tips of your left-hand fingers. (By the way, this is called "fretting" the notes.) This technique will create the best guitar tone and diminish any string buzzing.

- For the majority of your fretted notes, you should bring your left-hand thumb down so that it roughly lines up, on the back side of the guitar neck with your index finger.

- For some fretted notes, you will need to use a moderate amount of hand strength to make the notes sound.

Lesson 8: Secret to Guitar Success #2
Developing Good Practice Habits

One of the most important aspects of playing the guitar is forming good practice habits. Learning the guitar is a fun and creative endeavor; if you develop good practice habits you will make rapid progress with your playing. This will require a little bit of focus and a proactive attitude on your part. However, it will make a big difference for you.

Ideally, you should strive to practice around five to seven times per week (once per day) for about 20 to 40 minutes. If you have more time, that's great. However, it's best to spend your time practicing well (in an organized manner), rather than just spending a lot of time practicing. Along these lines, one of the most important facets of learning to play the guitar is having some continuity in your practice routine. So, even on days that you are extremely busy, try to take 10-15 minutes to work on your guitar playing. As best as you can, try to avoid missing more than three days of practicing in a row.

For the most positive results, you should strive to be organized with your practicing: have a plan for each practice session and have a few weekly goals. For example, a plan for a practice session might include spending 10 minutes on a technique or warm-up exercises, working on a lesson or two from this book for 20 minutes, and practicing a song for 15 minutes. Some examples for weekly goals might include working on four to five lessons from this book, practicing a song that you like, and spending 10 minutes a day on technique-improving exercises for your guitar playing. It should also be said that your weekly goals should not be too rigid (for example, "I *must* learn all of *Layla* this week.") or extremely lofty (for example, "This week, I'm going to learn 20 Foo Fighters' songs.").

Although letting your unconscious mind roam freely as you strum the guitar and noodle around with riffs and licks on the instrument is one important element to learning, discovery and improvement in music, try to keep this aspect of your playing to about 25% of your practicing. Sadly, many guitarists spend way too much time noodling around with their favorite sections of songs, ones that they are very comfortable playing. This often leads to guitarists falling into ruts with their playing (staying at the same level without improving). Though it is a lot of fun to noodle around on the guitar and play little riffs and licks, it's very important to be focused about your practicing and set clear goals for about 75% of your work time.

So, let's get started: Your lesson for today is to find a notebook or looseleaf binder that will be your practice journal. It does not have to be anything fancy or expensive. Take a few moments now to find one. If you do not have one around the house, buy one for a few dollars at a local store or online. This little investment will yield very positive results. Now, on the first page of the journal, write today's date, a lesson or two from this book that you would like to work on, and how much time you plan on spending on your guitar practice. You should continue this process for each day you practice. Some people like to cross off each task as they complete it. As well, it's often a good idea to write your next day's practice schedule at the end of your current day's practice session. This way, at some level, your mind will already be thinking about and planning for the next day's work; it's a good way to build and sustain momentum.

Lesson 9: Right-Hand Strumming Exercises & Counting Beats

Strumming the Guitar and Counting Beats: In this lesson we are going to work on right-hand strumming technique and also start learning how to count beats. Beats are the pulses in music that give it a clear rhythm. Most Rock music is based on groups of four beats. So, we count "One, Two, Three, Four". Each number equals one beat. Try this exercise, when you are listening to some Rock music (in the car, on your way to school or work, at home, etc.): Try to find the beats of the song that you are listening to by counting "One, Two, Three, Four" in your mind. Quite often in Rock music, there is an accent (a stronger pulse) on the first beat ("Beat One") of each group of four beats. Locating this strong first beat with your ear will help you.

Exercise 1: With the pick in your right hand strum down on the High-E string four times in a row. The High-E string is the thinnest string on your guitar. It is called the "High-E string" because it has the highest pitch ("sound"). Try this exercise 10 times in a row. Count out loud one beat for each down strum, like this: "One, Two, Three, Four".

(Count Beat One louder, since it is the strongest beat of the four.)

Down-Strum Pattern:

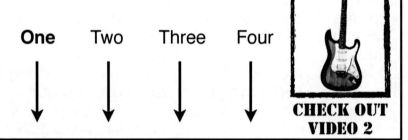

One   Two   Three   Four

CHECK OUT VIDEO 2

Exercise 2: With the pick in your right hand strum down on the both High-E string and the B string (the second string) together four times in a row. Use a gentle, downward motion, like you are petting a cat. Repeat this exercise 10 times in a row. Count "One, Two, Three, Four" for each down strum / beat. Try slightly varying the strength of your down strums. As you do this, listen to the change in the sound quality.

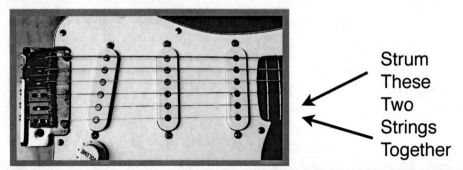

Strum These Two Strings Together

Exercise 3: Now, with the pick in your right hand strum down on the High-E string, the B string (the second string), and the G string (the third string) together four times in a row. Use a gentle, downward motion, like you are petting a cat. Repeat this exercise 10 times in a row. Count "One, Two, Three, Four" for each down strum / beat. Try slightly varying the strength of your down strums. As you do this, listen to the change in the sound quality.

Lesson 10: Easy Major Chords
C Major, F Major and G Major

In this lesson, we are going to learn three new chords (in easy-to-play format): C Major, F Major and G Major (see the diagrams).

For C Major, place your Index Finger on the First Fret of the Second String (the B String) and play Strings 1, 2 and 3 together.

For F Major, place your Index Finger on the First Fret of the Second String (the B String) and place your Middle Finger on the First Fret of the First String (the High-E String), and your Ring Finger on the Second Fret of the Third String (the G String). Play Strings 1, 2, and 3 together.

For G Major, place your Ring Finger on the Third Fret of the First String (the E String) and play Strings 1, 2, and 3 together.

Remember to place the tips of your left-hand fingers on the strings when you play chords.

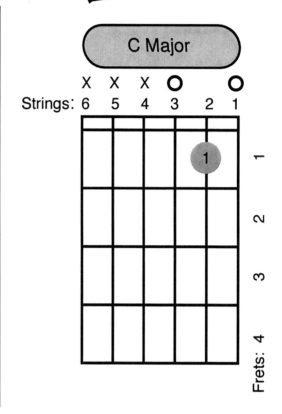

Please Note: The "X" symbol above the strings in these diagrams means don't play those strings. The "O" above the strings means play the string "open" (without any left-hand fingers).

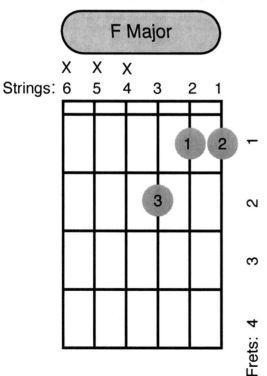

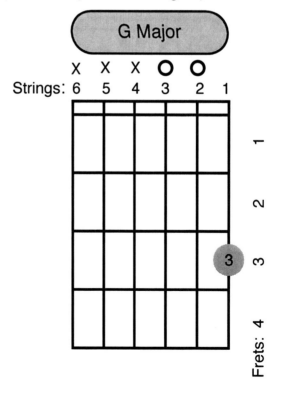

Lesson 11: Strumming Basics & *Three Chords and the Truth*

CHECK OUT VIDEO 3

In the previous lesson, you have had a chance to practice these three basic chord forms: C Major, F Major, and G Major. Now, let's put them into action in a song. In *Three Chords and the Truth*, there are three lines of music. A line of music can also be called a "system" (in musical terminology).

Each system in this song has four measures. Measures are groups of beats. Most Rock songs are grouped into measures that have four beats. In music terminology these four-beat measure groups are called "4/4 time". We'll go into more detail about this later, but for now, let's just count "1, 2, 3, 4" for each measure of *Three Chords and the Truth*.

For each measure of *Three Chords and the Truth,* play four down strums on the chord and count (aloud or in your mind "1, 2, 3, 4"). For example, for the first measure, play four down strums on the C chord and count one beat (aloud or in your mind) for each down strum.

Before playing the entire song, try switching between four down strums on the C chord and then four down strums on the F chord. After you are comfortable with alternating between these two chords, try switching between four down strums on the C chord and then four down strums on the G chord

Three Chords and the Truth

C	C	F	F
C	C	G	G
F	F	C	C

Lesson 12
Major Chords: Open Position

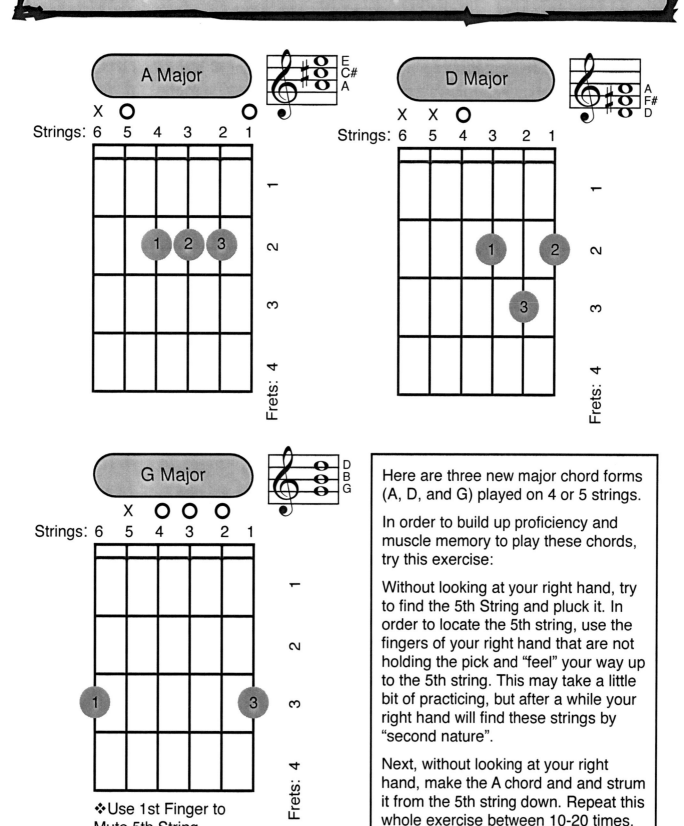

A Major

Strings: 6 5 4 3 2 1

E
C#
A

D Major

Strings: 6 5 4 3 2 1

A
F#
D

G Major

Strings: 6 5 4 3 2 1

D
B
G

❖Use 1st Finger to Mute 5th String

Here are three new major chord forms (A, D, and G) played on 4 or 5 strings.

In order to build up proficiency and muscle memory to play these chords, try this exercise:

Without looking at your right hand, try to find the 5th String and pluck it. In order to locate the 5th string, use the fingers of your right hand that are not holding the pick and "feel" your way up to the 5th string. This may take a little bit of practicing, but after a while your right hand will find these strings by "second nature".

Next, without looking at your right hand, make the A chord and and strum it from the 5th string down. Repeat this whole exercise between 10-20 times.

Lesson 13: Strumming and Chord Changes, Part 2

CHECK OUT VIDEO 4

Let's now start working on this tune that uses the three major chords that we learned from the previous lesson (D Major, G Major, and A Major). The D Major chord should be strummed from the 4th string (the D string) down through four strings: D, G, B, and the High E-string. This version of the G Major chord uses five strings: the Low-E, D, G, B, and High-E strings. You should use part of the pad of your index finger to mute the 5th string (the A string). If it is too much of a stretch to use the index finger for the G Major chord, you may use your thumb in its place. The A Major chord uses five strings: the A, D, G, B, and High-E strings.

For each measure of this song try to do this strumming pattern: Down Strum on the 1st Beat, Up Strum on the 2nd Beat, Down Strum on the 3rd Beat, Up Strum on the 4th Beat. Check out the diagram.

Practice each measure slowly and put one line (or system) together at a time.

Have Fun!

Down-Strum / Up-Strum Pattern:

One	Two	Three	Four
↓	↑	↓	↑

Tones

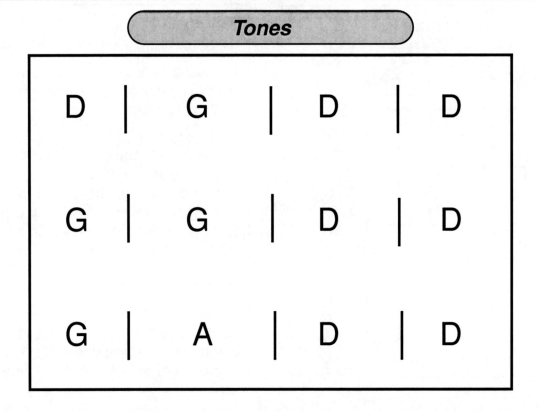

D	G	D	D
G	G	D	D
G	A	D	D

Lesson 14: Secret to Guitar Success #3 Patience & Longterm Perspective

Have patience and a longterm perspective: You are embarking on a grand and lifelong adventure in music. Through this journey, you will discover new perspectives on sound, communication, friendship, success, coordination, self confidence, concentration, memory, and determination. For the most part, this learning will be a step-by-step process, where your ability and understanding of music will move ahead at a gradual pace. At other times, your progress may suddenly leap ahead to another level in a flash of inspiration.

Whatever your goals in music may be, it's best to cultivate an attitude that music is a lifelong journey and process of creating and developing. As an artist, you should continue to explore and develop your musical voice. Life will take you along different paths and these will be reflected in your music making. Enjoy this adventure, especially if you are just beginning. You are like some explorer stepping onto the deck of your ship heading out from your land's port to find yet-unexplored, new places. Enjoy the journey!

In the next three lessons, we are going to look at three different methods for tuning your guitar. Each has its own benefit. So, you should spend time with all three methods to develop your skills. It may take a little while to cultivate your musical ear to hear the sometimes fine distinction between notes and strings that are in tune and ones that are a little bit out of tune. Just be patient with this skill. Over time and with practice you will be creating a very solid foundation for your musical hearing and understanding.

Playing in tune is a very important aspect of music and will make a huge difference in your sound, the development of your musical ear, and the respect that you will garner from fellow musicians and audience members. For most people, listening to someone play or sing out of tune elicits emotions ranging from annoyance to hilarity. If you have ever heard a violin concert performed by elementary students playing out of tune on screechy violins, you know what I mean. Although there is something charming about youngsters playing, you might not want to play a recording of the performance on your car stereo afterward.

So, the bottom line here is tuning is very important.

Lesson 15
Tuning the Guitar, Part 1

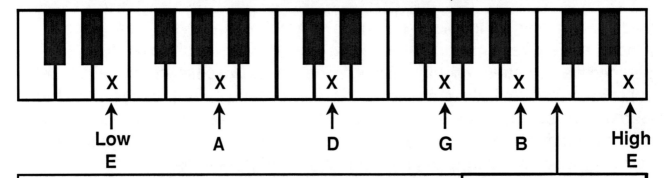

Low E   A   D   G   B   High E

Middle C (for the piano)

For this first method of tuning the guitar, you will need to have access to a piano, keyboard, or music app (like Garage Band, Logic, etc.) that has a mini piano keyboard feature. There are also a number of websites that have good, free virtual piano keyboards. You might try typing "piano keyboard" or "virtual piano keyboard" into a search engine like Google. A number of possible choices should show up in the search results.

In the chart above of the piano keyboard locate the piano key with the "X" that is labeled "Low E". Now on the piano, keyboard, or virtual "app" piano locate the key for "Low E" and play it. It should be located in the left-region of the piano keyboard. After you play the note on your keyboard, pluck the Low-E (the thickest) string of your guitar and listen to the sound. Try to match the sound of the keyboard, "Low-E note" by turning the tuning peg of your guitar either clockwise or counterclockwise.

As you get close to matching the pitch (sound) of the piano with your guitar, you will hear a kind of wavy / warbling sound as the guitar note aligns with the piano note. When the warbling / quavering stops and the notes are the same, you will be in unison ("in tune") with the piano note.

Now, locate the key in the piano chart above that is marked "A". Once you have done this, find and play the corresponding key for "A" on your piano keyboard (whether real or virtual). While the piano note for "A" is sounding pluck the 5th string of your guitar. This is the A string. Turn the tuning peg for the A string and match the pitch on your guitar with the pitch of the piano sound. Just as with the Low-E string, as you get closer to matching the "A" pitch in the piano with you guitar, you will hear a quavering in the pitch that goes from slow to fast as you tune in closer. Once the warbling stops and you have matched the "A" piano pitch, your "A" string will be in tune.

Repeat this same process of finding the note on your keyboard, playing it, and then matching it on your guitar for the next four strings: the D, G, B and High E (in order from thickest to thinnest). The notes / keys on your keyboard for this tuning method will go from left to right. Left is for the lower (deeper-sounding) notes on the piano. Right is for the higher sounds notes. This corresponds to the guitar strings going from thicker strings (with deeper sounds, like the Low-E string) to thinner strings (like the High E).

Lesson 16
Tuning the Guitar, Part 2

**CHECK OUT
VIDEO 5**

This next method for tuning can be used in conjunction with a tuning fork, pitch pipe, fixed-pitch instrument (like a piano, keyboard, harmonica, etc., if one is available), or just the guitar itself, if it is relatively in tune.

First, a little bit of background information: When the guitar is in standard tuning (that is, Low E, A, D, G, B, High E), a note on an adjacent thicker string fretted on the fifth fret (or in one case, the fourth fret) will match the note of its adjacent thinner open string in unison. In other words, when you place your finger on the 5th fret of the Low-E string (the 6th string), you will play the note "A". This is the same note as the open 5th String: the A string.

Give it a try. Put a finger on the 5th fret of the Low-E string and pluck the string. Now, play the 5th string (the A string) open (with no fingers pressing on a fret). It should be the same sound. If not, adjust the tuning peg for the A string to match the pitch of the fretted "A" note on the Low-E string (**see the video lesson on tuning for a demonstration**). Follow the same process for the A string and D string, as well as the D string and G string. (See chart below.) To tune the B string, play the note of the 4th fret of the G string (3rd string). This is the note "B", and then play the open B string. To tune the High-E string, play the 5th fret of the B string.

● Place your index finger down on the location of the black dot in the places indicated in the diagram below.

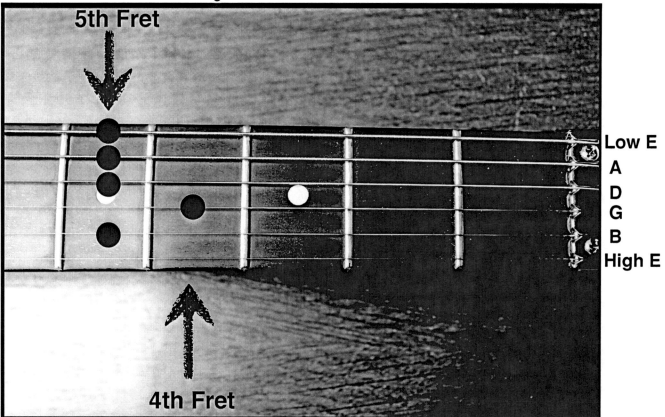

Lesson 17: Tuning the Guitar, Part 3 Portable, Electronic Guitar Tuners

Types of portable, electronic guitar tuners:
1. Clip-On Tuner 2. Smartphone App 3. Tablet App

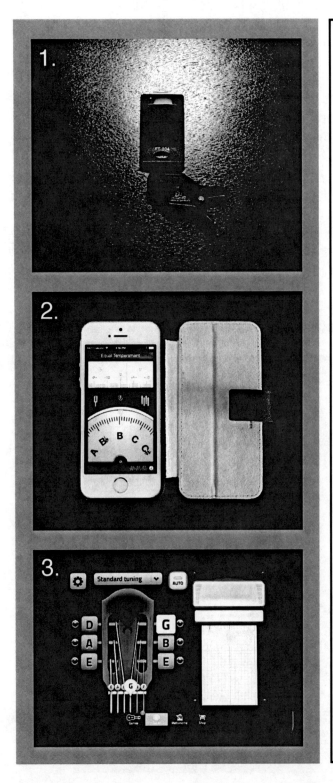

Electronic Tuners

Along with tuning the guitar by the methods previously detailed the last two lessons, it is also a good idea to get a portable electronic tuner. This is not a big rush; however, you might like to have one sometime over the next year or two, as you start playing music with family and friends, and also start to perform around your town and area.

There are several benefits to having a portable tuner. First off, you can tune the guitar quickly with a great deal of accuracy. You can also check your guitar's tuning after playing a few songs (during a practice session, band rehearsal, or performance). Next, you can tune the guitar accurately without access to a piano, keyboard, pitch pipe, tuning fork, or fixed-pitch tuning instrument or device.

These tuners come in all sorts of shapes and sizes. The most popular and practical are clip-on tuners (in the illustration at the top to the left) and guitar-tuner apps (in the middle and bottom illustrations to the left). They range in prices from free (for many of the Apps that will work on smartphones, tablets, and computers) to around twenty dollars. You can find them online or at your local music store.

Lesson 18: Gear Overview, Buying an Electric Guitar

These are the most important factors to consider when buying a guitar: the sound and variety of sounds the guitar can create, the ease of playing it and the way it fits your hands, how well it stays in tune, and the price (probably around $100-$200).

As you are trying out several guitars listen closely to the sound of each instrument and variety of sounds that you can get from them by turning their volume and tone knobs, as well as changing the position of the pickup toggle switches. (We will go into these techniques later in the book and videos.) If you are at a music store, you should also play the guitars through a few different amps, using both clean settings and distortion settings. This will give you a feeling for how they will sound in different musical contexts.

As mentioned above, you should be able to find a good, beginner-level electric guitar for around $100 to $200. In this price range, the level of quality varies considerably. So, try out many instruments and, before purchasing one, if possible, go shop with a family member or friend who has some music experience. He or she will be able to give you a second opinion on the sound and craftsmanship of the guitar.

Another element to consider while you are looking for guitars might be to try both used and new instruments. Unlike many electronic devices and vehicles, guitars often improve with age (both in terms of sound quality and playability). So, as you are looking for your first electric guitar, you might want to try out some used instruments.

As you are trying out the guitars start bending strings, up and down and use the tremolo / whammy bar, if the guitar has one. Then, after a minute or two of this bending and stretching of the strings, check to see if the guitar is still in tune. If the guitar stays in tune or requires a just a little bit of tuning, it's in good shape and will hold its tune. If, after bending and stretching the strings for a few minutes, the guitar is way out of tune, you should move on to the next candidate.

You should also check the action of the guitar. The action is the distance between the strings and the fretboard of the guitar. First, make sure that it is a comfortable action for your fingers. For many guitarists, if the action is too high the guitar is difficult to play. If the action is too low, it can be difficult to bend the strings. Also, make sure to check for any buzzing from the strings when you play notes. You should try playing notes on the guitar at the 3rd, 5th, 9th, 12th, 15th, and 19th frets and listen for any buzzing. If there is buzzing, the neck of the guitar may need a little adjustment. This can be done in the music shop. If the buzzing persists after an adjustment of the neck, it's time to go to the next candidate.

You should also understand that, in most cases, an electric guitar is a kind of hybrid instrument. Each electric guitar has a little bit of Frankenstein's monster in it (in a positive way). In other words, an electric guitar (for most Rock players) is a "constructed" instrument that can be modified, embellished, decorated, tinkered with, and even "mangled" (though I'm not an advocate of this) to fit the guitarist's style, musicality, and taste. After you buy an electric guitar, there are many free and inexpensive things that you can do to change its sound greatly. (We'll get into these later on in the book and videos).

Lesson 19: Gear Overview, Amp Basics, Part 1

There are two main categories of guitar amplification ("amps" for short): Tube amps and solid-state amps. Tube amps use vacuum tubes in both the pre-amplification and power amplification stages to amplify the guitar's sound. Solid-state amps use transistors for all stages. This can, and usually does, result in quite different tones between tube and solid-state amps. In general, it's better to look for a solid-state amp as your first guitar amplifier. Solid-state amps are lighter, sturdier, and a bit less expensive than tube amps. They also often come with built-in amp-modeling, which simulates many different types of amps, and built-in effects, like chorus, delay, reverb, flangers, and phasers. As you progress as a guitarist, you might then invest in a tube amp, which might put a little "dent in your wallet".

Here is a brief sketch of the way an amp works and how it affects the sound of your guitar:

You can think of a guitar amp as a device that takes the signal, which is sent from your electric guitar through a cable, and makes it louder (*much louder*). In a basic way, guitar amps have two stages: a weak signal goes from your instrument into the first stage, where it is processed and sent to the second stage that elevates it into a strong signal, which then comes out of the speakers.

The First Stage:

The first stage is called the "preamp". On many amps, you can control the level of the signal sent through this first stage. This control is called "gain", "distortion", or "drive", depending on the brand of the amplifier. As you turn the "gain" knob up on your amp, you are causing the amp to work harder. As the amp works harder to boost the signal it will start to distort the signal, giving it a "dirty" (rather than "clean") sound. Although, gain can be thought of as the input volume to the preamp stage, it is more of a tone control than a volume control. The gain setting determines how hard you're driving the preamp section of the amp. In other words, setting the gain control sets the level of distortion in your tone, regardless of how loud the final volume is set.

The Second Stage:

The second stage is the power amp section. This stage makes the overall sound louder or softer, giving power to the sound, rather than shaping it. On most amps, this knob is labelled "volume" or "master". On your own amp, you should try adjusting the balance between the gain knob and the volume knob. You will discover a wide array of new tones for your guitar just by raising or lowering these knobs in conjunction with each other.

EQ:

Another feature on most amps is the EQ. This stands for *equalization*. EQ is a way you can shape your sound by adding more treble or bass to the tone. For instance, if you want a smooth, milky lead tone inspired by Eric Clapton, you might lower the treble on your amp a bit and raise the bass knob slightly. If you want a crispy, punchy dirty rhythm sound for some Rolling Stones songs, you might boost the treble knob (and then raise the gain knob).

Lesson 20: Gear Overview: Amp Basics, Part 2

Solid-state amps deliver bright, clean, accurate sounds. They will respond quickly to your playing, and are more rugged than tube amps (requiring less maintenance). With advances in technology, many solid-state amps are loaded with a wide array of modeled-amp sounds and effects, giving you a lot of versatility. As well, solid-state amps from a given manufacturer tend to sound the same, which can be a benefit when you need a reliable, repeatable tone. They are also quite lighter—both in weight, and on the bank account—than tube amps.

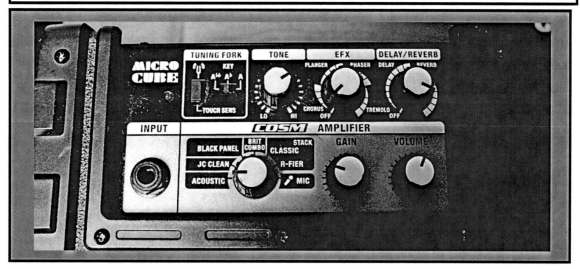

One-Channel, Solid-State Amp

Two-Channel Tube Amp

Tube amps have a certain indescribable "something" that makes them the most popular type of amp among seasoned guitarists and professionals. The sound of a tube amp has been described as "thick," "creamy," "fat," and "rich". This tone comes from the vacuum-tube technology that tube amps employ. Tube distortion is softer and a bit fuller than solid-state amp distortion. On the downside, tube amps are also more expensive, both initially, and when it comes to maintenance, by a few hundred to a few thousand dollars, than equivalent solid-state amps. They can also be quite heavy to carry around. It's important, as a beginner Rock guitarist that you play music with family and friends often; this will help you improve as a musician. With this in mind, it's a lot easier to carry a solid-state amp than a tube amp to a rehearsal.

Lesson 21: Check Out These Rock Songs That Have Major Chords

Take a little time now and listen to the following rock songs that use major chords. You might check out YouTube or the artists' websites for free recordings and performance videos. Listen to the guitar parts in each song and try to pick up ideas and sounds for strumming chords, which you can then add your own playing. Take a moment and listen to these songs in an active way, focusing on the guitar sound for each band and artist.

An important part of developing as a guitarist and musician is to continually listen to new songs. If you hear something that you like in an artist's guitar playing, try to find a way to imitate it and incorporate it into your own playing.

Here are a few:

• Tom Petty: *Free Falling*

• The Beatles: *Hey Jude*

• Jimi Hendrix: *The Wind Cries Mary*

• Rush: *Closer to the Heart*

• Foo Fighters: *Walk*

• Bruce Springsteen: *Born to Run*

• U2: *Where the Streets Have No Name*

• Eric Johnson: *Nothing Can Keep Me from You*

Lesson 22: Chapter 1 Overview
What We Have Learned

- Secret to Guitar Success #1: Have a Positive Attitude, Enjoy the Process, and Have Fun

- Types of Guitars: Acoustic, Solid-Body Electric & Hollow-Body Electric

- Parts of the Acoustic Guitar

- Parts of the Electric Guitar

- An Explanation of the Parts of the Guitar

- The Names of the Strings from Low to High: Low E, A, D, G, B, High E

- Holding the Guitar Pick / Right-Hand Exercises

- Secret to Guitar Success #2: Developing Good Practice Habits

- Right-Hand Strumming & Counting Beats

- Easy Major Chords: C, F & G

- Strumming Basics & *Three Chords & the Truth*

- Major Chords in Open Position: A, D & G

- Strumming and Chord Changes, Part 2

- Secret to Guitar Success #3: Patience & A Longterm Perspective

- Tuning the Guitar, Part 1: With a Piano or Keyboard

- Tuning the Guitar, Part 2: Using the 5th- & 4th-Fret Method

- Tuning the Guitar, Part 3: Electronic Tuners

- Gear Overview: Buying an Electric Guitar

- Gear Overview: Amp Basics, Part 1: How Amps Work

- Gear Overview: Amp Basics, Part 2: Tube Amps & Solid-State Amps

CHAPTER TWO: ROCK GUITAR BASICS

Lesson 23: Tablature Basics

Guitar tablature (or TAB for short) is a notation system that graphically indicates guitar fingering, rather than the actual notes and pitches to be played. In other words, TAB shows you the exact location on strings and frets where you will need to play, but it does not tell you the actual notes (for example, "Eb", G, B) or the rhythms and durations of what you will be playing. Tablature is a good initial "shorthand" notation, especially if you are already familiar with a song, but it might have some drawbacks if you solely rely on it to learn music. For this book, we will use tablature and video examples to show the licks and exercises. Later on in your guitar studies, you might like to learn to read standard notation, which will give you a more accurate representation of what's going on in music.

Here is how it works: The thickest string (Low-E string) is the bottom line of the tablature staff and the thinnest string (High-E string) is the top line of the tablature staff. So, the higher lines on the staff represent the higher-pitched guitar strings and the lower lines on the tablature staff represent the lower-pitched guitar strings. A note on the guitar is indicated by placing a number on one of the lines of the tablature staff. The number represents which fret to place your finger on and the line indicates which string to play. However, tablature does not indicate how long to play the note, which left-hand finger to use, or how loud to play the note. As mentioned above, it does not indicate the actual name of the note ("pitch") that you are playing. It does, though, sometimes indicate other qualities of the note--for example, if you are supposed to bend the note, play a pull off or hammer on, or give vibrato (more about all of these techniques later on in the book).

Chords are represented by placing the numbers on top of each other on the TAB staff. The number zero indicates that you should play an open string.

One last thing, even though tablature has been around for centuries (it was used frequently in the Renaissance), there is not a one-hundred-percent set system for the notation. So, you might see slight variations among the TAB versions in a number of Rock songbooks or online TAB-versions of songs.

Tablature Example of the C Major Chord from Lesson 10
(See the Chord chart on Lesson 10)

```
——————————————0———————————————— High-E String (1st String)
——————————————1———————————————— B String (2nd String)
——————————————0———————————————— G String (3rd String)
———————————————————————————————— D String (4th String)
———————————————————————————————— A String (5th String)
———————————————————————————————— Low-E String (6th String)
```

Lesson 24: Alternate Picking

Here are three alternate-picking exercises (in tablature / TAB format) to improve your right-hand picking technique. Repeat each exercise at a comfortable tempo for between 1 and 2 minutes. If your hands start to feel tired, just shake them out and take a break for a while.

⊓ : This symbol stands for a downstroke.

V : This symbol stands for an upstroke.

⊓ V ⊓ V ⊓ V ⊓ V

```
0 1 0 1 0 1 0 1 ———— High-E String (1st String)
———————————————————— B String (2nd String)
———————————————————— G String (3rd String)
———————————————————— D String (4th String)
———————————————————— A String (5th String)
———————————————————— Low-E String (6th String)
```

⊓ V ⊓ V ⊓ V ⊓ V

```
1 2 1 2 1 2 1 2 ———— High-E String (1st String)
———————————————————— B String (2nd String)
———————————————————— G String (3rd String)
———————————————————— D String (4th String)
———————————————————— A String (5th String)
———————————————————— Low-E String (6th String)
```

⊓ V ⊓ V ⊓ V ⊓ V ⊓

```
1 2 3 1 2 3 1 2 3 ——— 1st String
———————————————————— 2nd String
———————————————————— 3rd String
———————————————————— 4th String
———————————————————— 5th String
———————————————————— 6th String
```

CHECK OUT VIDEO 6

Lesson 25
Major Chords: Open Position

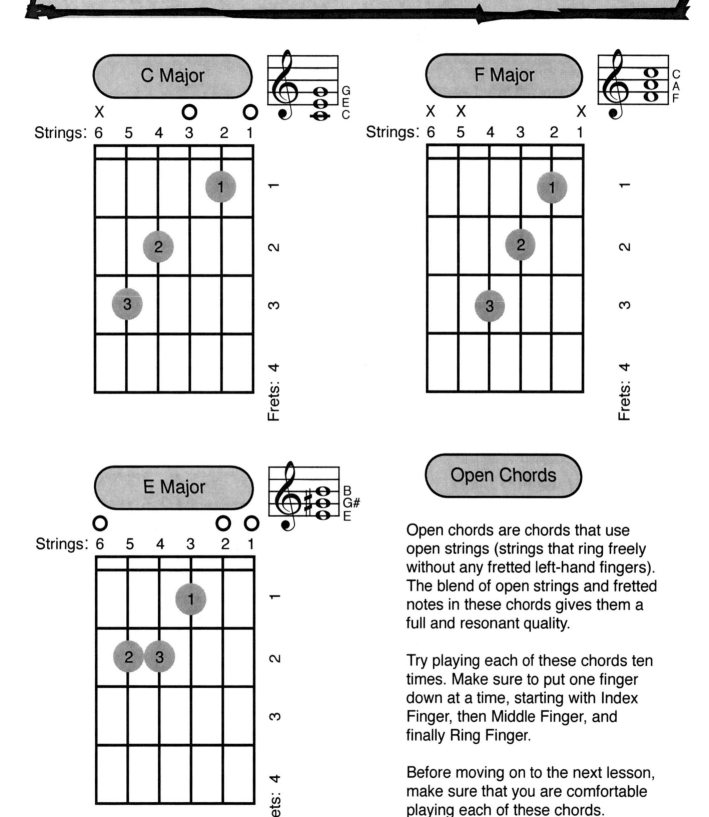

C Major

Strings: 6 5 4 3 2 1

Frets: 4

F Major

Strings: 6 5 4 3 2 1

Frets: 4

E Major

Strings: 6 5 4 3 2 1

Frets: 4

Open Chords

Open chords are chords that use open strings (strings that ring freely without any fretted left-hand fingers). The blend of open strings and fretted notes in these chords gives them a full and resonant quality.

Try playing each of these chords ten times. Make sure to put one finger down at a time, starting with Index Finger, then Middle Finger, and finally Ring Finger.

Before moving on to the next lesson, make sure that you are comfortable playing each of these chords.

Lesson 26: Strumming Techniques with Open Chords

Exercise 1: For this song, try two different strumming styles. For the first one, do all down strums. Count out loud or in your head one beat for each down strum, like this: "One, Two, Three, Four".

(Count Beat One louder, since it is the strongest beat of the four.)

Down-Strum Pattern:

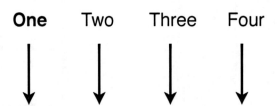

One   Two   Three   Four

For the second strumming style, try to do this pattern: Down Strum on the 1st Beat, Up Strum on the 2nd Beat, Down Strum on the 3rd Beat, Up Strum on the 4th Beat. Check out the diagram.

Practice each measure slowly and put one line (or system) together at a time.

Have Fun!

Down-Strum / Up-Strum Pattern:

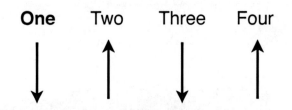

One   Two   Three   Four

Zapped

CHECK OUT VIDEO 7

C	C	F	F
C	C	F	F
F	F	C	C

Lesson 27: Secret to Guitar Success #4: Using a Metronome

A lot of beginning musicians overlook the importance of practicing with a metronome. A metronome is a mechanical or electronic device that keeps a steady beat. You can change the speed of the beats, which in music is called the "tempo", on all metronomes to allow for slower or faster pulses of rhythm.

As soon as possible, you should incorporate a metronome into your practicing for guitar techniques and songs. This will help build and solidify your internal rhythm, so that when you play with other people you fit perfectly in the groove with the bassist and drummer. Playing in time with other musicians is as important as playing in tune. If you are out of sync with the grove of the music it is similar to playing in the wrong key. The music will sound awkward and disjointed.

You can find a number of free or inexpensive metronome apps online. These will work on your computer, tablet and smartphone. There are also a wide assortment of digital metronomes that you can purchase. Many of these can be found online or at your local music store for around ten dollars.

Lesson 28: Secret to Guitar Success #5: Playing with Other People

As soon as you learn a few songs that you can play comfortably, you should ask a friend or family member to play music with you. This will be a positive and new experience, which will make you a better musician. Since playing music is like having a conversation, you will become more fluent and expressive with your guitar playing. You will also have new ideas about playing, which will be influenced by the other person or people in your jam session. Even though it may take a little courage to reach out to someone to play, it is well worth the effort.

Lesson 29: Music Theory: What are Intervals?, Part 1

- In music, the distance between any 2 notes is called an "Interval".
- Intervals can be played at the same time, for example, if you press down two guitar notes, or they can be played one after the other, for example, if you play the note "C" and then the note "D".
- The easiest way to understand intervals is to look at the illustration of the piano keyboard. Locate Middle C and then find the bracket marked "2nd" connecting it to the note "D". This interval is called a 2nd. **Check out the chart below.**
- Next, find Middle C and the note "E" in the chart below. This interval is called a 3rd.
- Now, on your guitar, play the open High-E String. Then, play the 1st fret of the high E String. This is a minor second (or half step) interval. Listen to its sound character.
- Next, on your guitar, play the open High-E String. Then, play the 2nd fret of the high E String. This is a major second (or whole step) interval. Listen to its sound character.
- Now, on your guitar, play the open High-E String. Then, play the 3rd fret of the high E String. This is a minor third interval. Listen to the sound character of the interval.

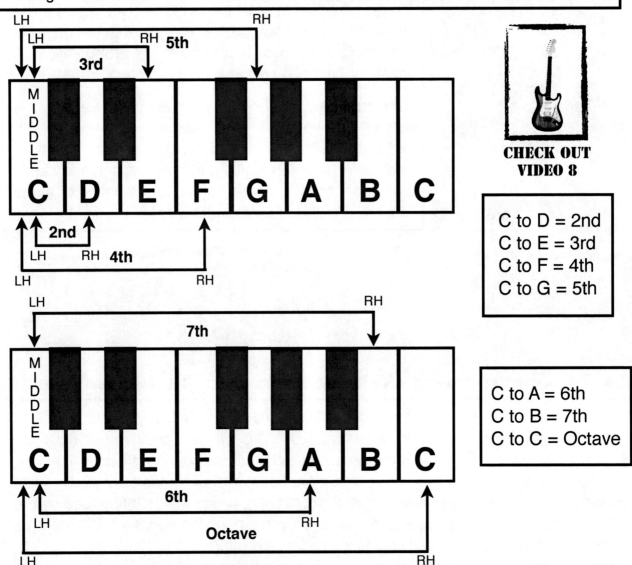

CHECK OUT VIDEO 8

C to D = 2nd
C to E = 3rd
C to F = 4th
C to G = 5th

C to A = 6th
C to B = 7th
C to C = Octave

Lesson 30: Music Theory: What are Intervals?, Part 2

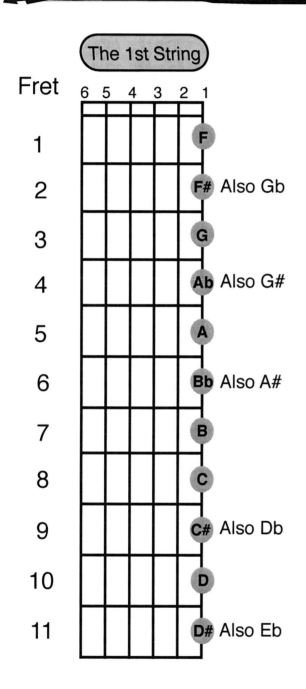

The 1st String

Fret   6 5 4 3 2 1

1   F
2   F# Also Gb
3   G
4   Ab Also G#
5   A
6   Bb Also A#
7   B
8   C
9   C# Also Db
10 D
11 D# Also Eb

"Intervals" are the distances between two notes in music. For example, the distance between the notes "E" and "F" on your fretboard (the open E string and the 1st fret of the E string) is an interval, which is called a "minor second".

Here are some common names for intervals: minor second, major third, minor third, perfect 4th, perfect 5th, and octave. While these names may seem a bit technical, they just indicate the space between 2 notes. Try playing the intervals listed in the chart below on on the high E string on your guitar and listen to the difference in sounds.

Intervals on 1 String

1. Open String then 1st Fret = Minor 2nd
2. Open String then 2nd Fret = Major 2nd
3. Open String then 3rd Fret = Minor 3rd
4. Open String then 4th Fret = Major 3rd
5. Open String then 5th Fret = Perfect 4th
6. Open String then 6th Fret = Diminished 5th
7. Open String then 7th Fret = Perfect 5th
8. Open String then 8th Fret = Minor 6th
9. Open String then 9th Fret = Major 6th
10. Open String then 10 Fret = Minor 7th
11. Open String then 11th Fret = Major 7th
12. Open String then 12th Fret = Octave

You might recognize some of these intervals from famous movie soundtracks. For example, the "Jaws Theme" uses a minor second. A perfect fifth is outlined by the first two notes of the "Star Wars Theme".

Lesson 31: Minor Chords In Open Position

Minor chords are three-note chords that tend to have a "darker" or "sadder" sound than major chords. Most upbeat and happy Rock songs use major chords, think of *I'm Walking on Sunshine* or *Here Comes the Sun*. Many sadder, somber, or moody Rock songs use minor chords--for example, *Paint It Black, Stairway to Heaven,* and *The River*.

Being able to play minor chords, will give you access to a broader range of song repertoire. It will also help you to write songs that have a wider emotional range. Over the next few lessons, we are going to look at some minor chords.

For the A Minor chord, place your Index Finger on the 1st fret of the 2nd string, place your Ring Finger on the 2nd fret of the 3rd string, and place your Middle Finger on the 2nd fret of the 4th string. Then, strum from the 5th string down through the 1st string.

For the D Minor chord, place your Index Finger on the 1st fret of the 1st string, place your Ring Finger on the 3rd fret of the 2nd string, and place your Middle Finger on the 2nd fret of the 3rd string. Then, strum from the 4th string down through the 1st string.

In the charts below, "R" stands for the root of the chord, "3" stands for the 3rd of the chord, and "5" stands for the 5th of the chord.

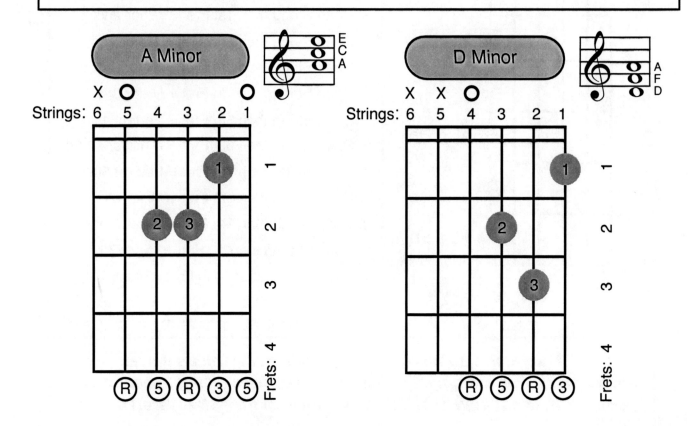

Lesson 32: Major & Minor Chords
House of the Rising Sun

CHECK OUT VIDEO 9

House of the Rising Sun is a classic Blues Rock song that was made popular by The Animals in the 1960s. Artists as diverse as Tommy Emmanuel and Christina Aguilera have performed *House of the Rising Sun*. It is a great example of a rock song that effectively blends major and minor chords.

The song is in 3/4 time (or "time signature"), which is a bit unusual for Rock music. You will need to strum three times for each chord in each measure. To do this effectively, it's best to count aloud or in your head, "1, 2, 3, 1, 2, 3", as you strum the chords.

If you are having any trouble remembering the chords forms for this song, look back to the chord lessons from earlier in this book.

There is a Jam-Track, Play-Along video for this song. ***Have Fun!***

House of the Rising Sun

Chord:	Am	C	D	F
	There is a	house in	New Or-	leans they
Strum:	1 2 3	1 2 3	1 2 3	1 2 3

Chord:	Am	C	E	E
	call the	ris- ing	sun.	It's
Strum:	1 2 3	1 2 3	1 2 3	1 2 3

Chord:	Am	C	D	F
	been the	ruin of	many poor	souls and
Strum:	1 2 3	1 2 3	1 2 3	1 2 3

Chord:	Am	E	Am	Am
	Lord, I	know I'm	one.	
Strum:	1 2 3	1 2 3	1 2 3	1 2 3

Lesson 33:
Rock Technique: Slides

**CHECK OUT
VIDEO 10**

Slides are a great technique to add nuance and new colors to your guitar playing. Sliding is a very popular guitar technique and is relatively easy to master. Basically, it just entails sliding one of your left-hand fingers up or down the fretboard between notes. This glissando effect will give your playing a vocal quality, like a great Rock or Blues singer.

You may hear a little buzzing or squeaking sound from the strings as you are sliding up or down. This is completely normal and is often part of the effect of the technique. Later on in the book and videos, you will learn about vibrato technique. When you combine slides and vibrato, your musicality will go to new levels of expression.

This is the basic technique for playing slides on the guitar: First, fret a note, pluck the string, then slide your left-hand finger to another fret (up or down) on the same string, without picking the string again. Try to let the notes ring out as you slide up or down the string. For a small slide, you can just go up or down one fret. Give this a try. For a bigger slide, try plucking a note and sliding your finger five or six frets up or down. Do you hear the difference in sound? Now, try sliding up to a new note and then slide back to the original fret.

Also, as you are sliding, only press down on the string as much as is needed to keep the note ringing. If you press down too hard, it will hurt your finger and make it difficult to slide up and down the fretboard.

Below, is a slide lick. On the High-E string (the 1st string), slide up from the 1st fret to the 3rd fret. Then, slide down from the 3rd fret to the 1st fret. Listen to the effect. Try playing it slowly a few times. Slide to the notes in a leisurely manner. Once you have that down, try sliding into the notes quickly.

Slides are often indicated with a diagonal line and a slur marker between the notes.

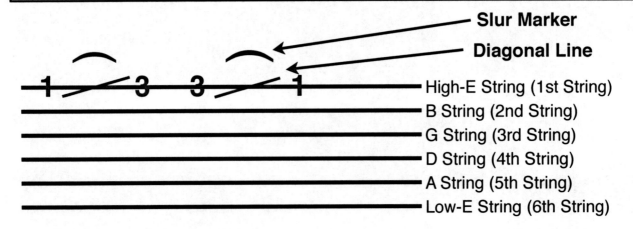

Lesson 34: Licks That Use Slide Techniques

Try out these three guitar licks that use slides. In the first one, you will slide between the 3rd and 5th frets on the 2nd string (the B string) and also play the open High-E string and the open B string. The second and third examples are on the 1st string. They combine the sounds of slides and open strings. As you learn these guitar licks, and all of the licks in this book, experiment with the sound of each lick (change the speed of your playing, add a few notes here and there, etc.). A big part of becoming a good guitar player is articulating each note in a meaningful way. So, have fun discovering new ways to play each one of the guitar licks.

CHECK OUT VIDEO 11

1.

```
High-E String (1st String) ----------0-----------0---------
B String (2nd String) -----3 / 5-----5 \ 3-----0---
G String (3rd String) -------------------------------------
D String (4th String) -------------------------------------
A String (5th String) -------------------------------------
Low-E String (6th String) ---------------------------------
```

2.

```
High-E String (1st String) --5 \ 3--0--5 \ 3--0---
B String (2nd String) -------------------------------------
G String (3rd String) -------------------------------------
D String (4th String) -------------------------------------
A String (5th String) -------------------------------------
Low-E String (6th String) ---------------------------------
```

3.

```
High-E String (1st String) --2 / 3--0--2 / 1--0---
B String (2nd String) -------------------------------------
G String (3rd String) -------------------------------------
D String (4th String) -------------------------------------
A String (5th String) -------------------------------------
Low-E String (6th String) ---------------------------------
```

***As a side note, the slide technique we are going over in this lesson and the previous lesson just involves the fingers. There is another group of techniques, which use a simple device (called "a slide"); this device is a small, 3-inch tube (made of metal or glass) that is placed on a finger of the left hand. Duane Allman and Derek Trucks are among some of the great slide-guitar players. You might check out some videos of their performances.

Lesson 35: Open Position E Minor & B Minor Chords

In this lesson we are going to look at two new minor chords: E Minor and B Minor.

For the E Minor chord, place your Index Finger on the 2nd fret of the 5th string and place your Middle Finger on the 2nd fret of the 4th string. Then, strum from the 6th string down through the 1st string. Since this chord uses all six strings, it has a full, resonant sound. Try doing a down strum and listen to the sound. Then, try playing an up strum. Listen to the way it sounds if you strum softly. Then, give a quick, loud strum and listen to the way it sounds. Try this strumming technique with the other chords that you have learned from the book.

For the B Minor chord, place your Index Finger on the 2nd fret of the 1st string, place your Middle Finger on the 3rd fret of the 2nd string, place your Ring Finger on the 4th fret of the 4th string, and place your Pinky Finger on the 4th fret of the 3rd string. Then, strum from the 4th string down through the 1st string. Since this chords uses four fingers, it may take you a little while to learn. So, be patient and place one finger down at a time, going from finger one to finger four in order. Little by little, you will gain proficiency playing the chord.

In the charts below, "R" stands for the root of the chord, "3" stands for the 3rd of the chord, and "5" stands for the 5th of the chord.

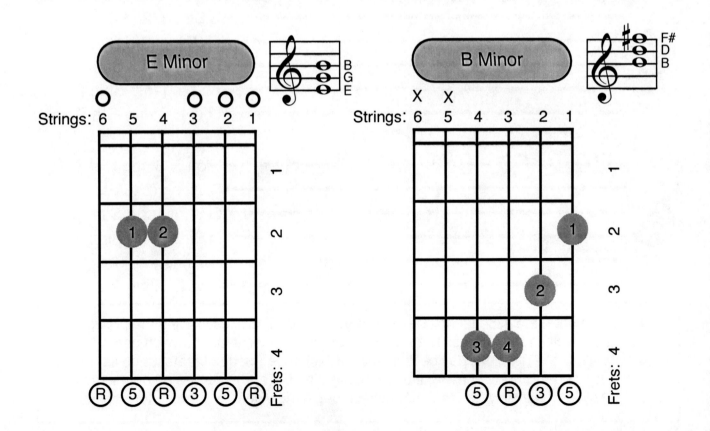

Lesson 36: More Minor Chords In Open Position

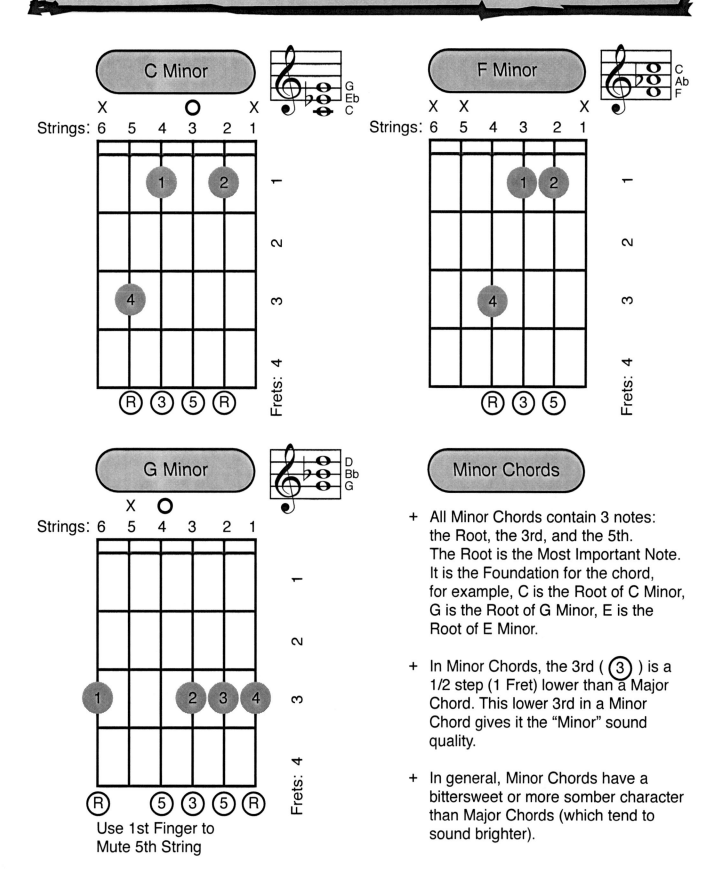

C Minor

G
Eb
C

Strings: 6 5 4 3 2 1

X O X

1 2

4

Frets: 1 2 3 4

(R) (3) (5) (R)

F Minor

C
Ab
F

Strings: 6 5 4 3 2 1

X X X

1 2

4

Frets: 1 2 3 4

(R) (3) (5)

G Minor

D
Bb
G

Strings: 6 5 4 3 2 1

X O

1 2 3 4

Frets: 1 2 3 4

(R) (5) (3) (5) (R)

Use 1st Finger to
Mute 5th String

Minor Chords

+ All Minor Chords contain 3 notes:
  the Root, the 3rd, and the 5th.
  The Root is the Most Important Note.
  It is the Foundation for the chord,
  for example, C is the Root of C Minor,
  G is the Root of G Minor, E is the
  Root of E Minor.

+ In Minor Chords, the 3rd ((3)) is a
  1/2 step (1 Fret) lower than a Major
  Chord. This lower 3rd in a Minor
  Chord gives it the "Minor" sound
  quality.

+ In general, Minor Chords have a
  bittersweet or more somber character
  than Major Chords (which tend to
  sound brighter).

Lesson 37: Music Theory: Major & Minor Chords

Overview

Chords are groups of notes played at the same time. What gives each chord its particular character are the specific notes (for example, C, A, F#, etc.) and the positioning / distance of the notes from one another (the intervals of the chord).

We are now going to look at the intervals that make up major and minor chords. All major and minor chords follow these same basic principles. So, it is important that you commit these ideas to memory. When you are playing a gig or at a rehearsal, a keyboard or sax player might ask you to bring out the 3rd the the chord. Your lead singer might want you to change a chord from major to minor.

Major & Minor Chords

+ All Major & Minor Chords contain 3 notes: the Root, the 3rd, and the 5th.

+ In Major Chords the distance between the Root and the 3rd is made up of 2 Major 2nds.

+ In Minor Chords the distance between the Root and the 3rd is made up of 1 Major 2nd and 1 Minor 2nd.

Major
— 3rd
Major 2nd
Major 2nd
Root

Minor
— 3rd
Minor 2nd
Major 2nd
Root

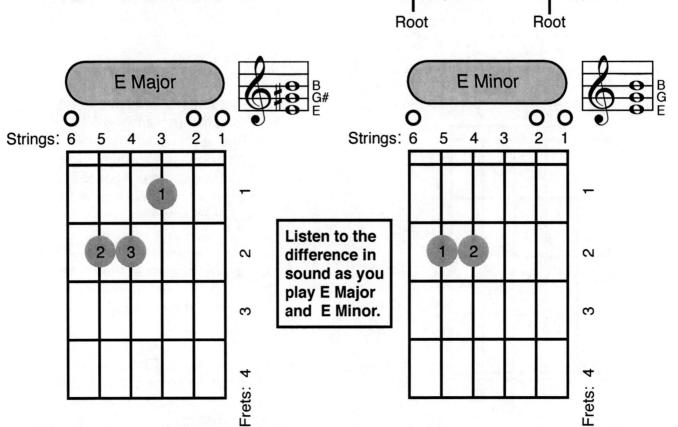

E Major — B G# E

E Minor — B G E

Strings: 6 5 4 3 2 1

Listen to the difference in sound as you play E Major and E Minor.

Frets: 1 2 3 4

Lesson 38: Gear Overview
Pickups and Toggle Switches

Electric guitar pickups take a string's vibration and turn the vibration into an electrical signal that can be sent through an amp or mixer. Although there are a wide variety of pickups available, they fall mainly into two broad categories: Single-Coil Pickups and Double-Coil Pickups (also called "humbuckers").

Until the mid 1950s, all pickups were single coil. However, though, single-coil pickups sound great, they are often quite noisy, transmitting an electrical hum and buzz along with the sound of the vibrating strings. In the mid 1950s, Gibson Guitars created a pickup configuration that combined two single-coil pickups into one. The way that they wired the pickups cancelled (or "bucked") the electrical hum. These double-coil pickups became known as "humbuckers".

In terms of the sound quality, single-coil pickups tend to be brighter and crisper, with greater note definition between strings, while double-coil pickups ("humbuckers") often tend to be a bit louder, darker and deeper.

CHECK OUT VIDEO 12

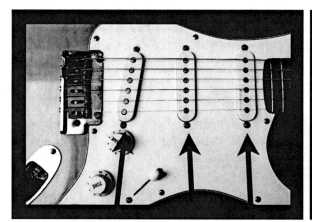

Single-Coil Pickups &
Five-Position Toggle Swich

Humbucker Pickups &
Three-Position Toggle Swich

On your guitar, find the pickup toggle switch. It will most likely either have three positions or five positions. These positions activate the different pickup combinations. If you have a five-position switch, the rightmost position will activate the bridge pickup and the leftmost position will activate the neck pickup. The middle position on the toggle switch will activate the middle pickup. The two other toggle-switch positions blend either the bridge and middle pickups or the neck and middle pickups. A three-position toggle switch is similar. However, the middle position just blends the neck and bridge pickups. Try playing some chords or licks on your guitar with different pickups activated. Listen to the difference in sound between the neck and bridge pickups.

Lesson 39: Music Theory
Learning the First-String Notes

The 1st String

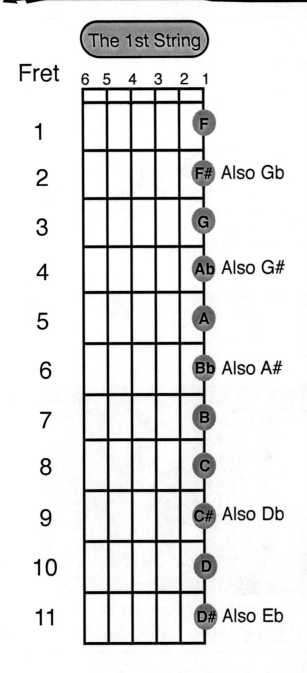

Fret						
	6	5	4	3	2	1
1						F
2						F# Also Gb
3						G
4						Ab Also G#
5						A
6						Bb Also A#
7						B
8						C
9						C# Also Db
10						D
11						D# Also Eb

Notes on the 1st String

Now that you are make progress in your playing, it's time to start learning the notes of the fretboard. This is a very important skill to have as a guitarist, even if you are not interested in learning how to read music. If you don't know the notes of the fretboard, when someone asks you to play a certain note, for instance "G", you won't know where to find it. Along these lines, not knowing the notes of the fretboard will seriously limit your ability to communicate with other musicians. So, let's get to work learning these note names.

We'll start with the notes of the 1st string (the High-E string). The note "E" is the open string.

1. Find the note "G" on your guitar and play it. Check the chart on the left to see if you are on the right fret.
2. Find the note "B" on your guitar and play it. Check the chart on the left to see if you are on the right fret.
3. Find the note "F" on your guitar and play it. Check the chart on the left to see if you are on the right fret.
4. Find the note "D" on your guitar and play it. Check the chart on the left to see if you are on the right fret.

Repeat this exercise each day, using all of the notes listed in the chart on the left, until you can find the notes with ease.

As an added benefit, once you have learned the notes for the High-E string, you will also have learned the note names for the Low-E string (the 6th string). The note names are on the same frets for both strings, just two octaves apart. Play the Low-E string open and then the High-E string open; you will hear the difference in sound clearly.

Lesson 40: Power Chords

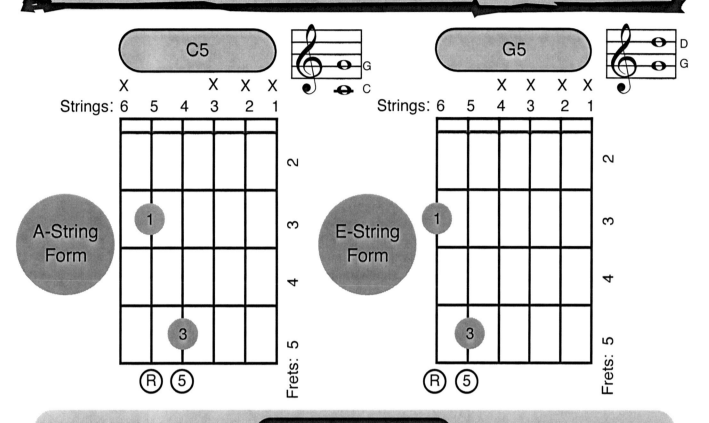

| C5 | | | | | |
| X | | X | X | X | |
Strings: 6 5 4 3 2 1

A-String Form

G

C

G5

X X X X
Strings: 6 5 4 3 2 1

E-String Form

D

G

Power Chords

- Power Chords, in general, are 2-note chords that are used in guitar-oriented music that has a driving beat.

- Power Chords are made up of the Root and 5th of the chord. The 3rd of the chord is usually not played. The abbreviation for most power chords is the Root note plus the number "5". For example, a "C" power chord, would be written like this: C5. A "G" power chord would be written like this: G5.

- The two chords depicted above are the most common forms of power chords. These forms can be moved up and down the neck of the guitar. So, you do not have to change left-hand finger positioning if you are going from one power chord to the next, if they are on the same string.

Lesson 41: *House of the Rising Sun*: Power Chord Version

Let's now play *House of the Rising Sun* with power chords. The two-string power chords that we are going to use for this song are only on the 6th and 5th strings (the Low-E string and the A string). Use the **E-String Form** of the power chord from the lesson on the previous page. You will <u>not</u> need to change your finger placement to play the power chords for the song. You will only need to shift your hand position up and down along the neck.

- **For A5 place your index finger on the 5th fret of the 6th string.**

- **For C5 place your index finger on the 8th fret of the 6th string.**

- **For D5 place your index finger on the 10th fret of the 6th string.**

- **For E5 place your index finger on the 12th fret of the 6th string.**

- **For F5 place your index finger on the 1st fret of the 6th string**.

This Classic Rock song is in 3/4 time; so, strum each chord three times per measure. To get different sounds, try moving your pickup toggle switch to different positions. The neck pickup will give you a bluesy bass-oriented sound. The bridge pickup will give you more crunch.

House of the Rising Sun

Chord:	A5			C5			D5			F5		
	There	is	a	house	in		New	Or-		leans	they	
Strum:	1	2	3	1	2	3	1	2	3	1	2	3

Chord:	A5			C5			E5			E5		
		call	the	ris-		ing	sun.					It's
Strum:	1	2	3	1	2	3	1	2	3	1	2	3

Chord:	A5			C5			D5			F5		
		been	the	ruin	of		many	poor		souls	and	
Strum:	1	2	3	1	2	3	1	2	3	1	2	3

Chord:	A5			E5			A5			A5		
		Lord,	I	know	I'm		one.					
Strum:	1	2	3	1	2	3	1	2	3	1	2	3

Lesson 42: Changing the Guitar Strings

Here is a nine-step method for changing your guitar strings:

Before starting, it's best to have a set of pliers and a string winder.

Step 1: Separate your strings and put them in order. You will be changing them one at a time.

Step 2: Loosen <u>one</u> string and snip it with your pliers. Do <u>not</u> cut all of your strings at once.

Step 3: Depending on your guitar model, feed the new string through the bridge from the back or side.

Step 4: Measure out a finger length of slack for the guitar string.

Step 5: Gently feed the string through the hole in the tuning peg.

Step 6: Make a downward-pointing fold in the string.

Step 7: Using the string winder, turn the tuning peg clockwise. This will tighten the string.

Step 8: Check to make sure that the string is wound upon itself. This will improve the tuning.

Step 9: Once the string is at the correct pitch, snip the excess wire with your pliers.

Lesson 43: Check Out These Songs that Use Minor Chords

Take a little time now and listen to the following Rock songs that use minor chords. You might check out YouTube or the artists' websites for free recordings and performance videos. Listen to the guitar parts in each song and try to pick up ideas and sounds for strumming chords, which you can then add your own playing. Take a moment and listen to these songs in an active way, focusing on the guitar sound for each band and artist.

Here are a few:

• Santana: *Smooth*

• The Beatles: *Eleanor Rigby*

• Aerosmith: *Dream On*

• Jimi Hendrix: *Little Wing*

• Van Halen: *Ain't Talkin' 'Bout Love*

• Bruce Springsteen: *The River*

• Dire Straits: *Sultans of Swing*

• Adele: *Rolling In the Deep*

• Led Zeppelin: *Stairway to Heaven*

Lesson 44: Licks Inspired by Great Rock Guitarists: Angus Young

Here are two alternate-picking exercises (inspired by Angus Young) to improve your right-hand picking technique. Repeat each exercise at a comfortable tempo for between 1 and 2 minutes. If your hand or wrist starts to feel tired, just shake it out and take a break for a while.

CHECK OUT VIDEO 13

Let's look at some open-string licks in the style of Angus Young of the Australian Rock group, AC/DC. Angus Young is a great Rock guitarist. Among his many stylistic trademarks are his use of power chords, string bends, rapid-fire blues lines, rhythmic groves, and open-string licks. You might check out some of these ACDC songs that feature these elements: *Back in Black, For Those About to Rock, Dirty Deeds Done Dirt Cheap,* and *Highway to Hell.*

These two licks are based on something Angus Young might play in *Back In Black*. They involve playing on open strings and primarily use the first, second, and third strings (High-E string, B string, and G string, respectively). They work well over an E Minor Chord or if you are playing a song in the key of E Minor. ***Have Fun!***

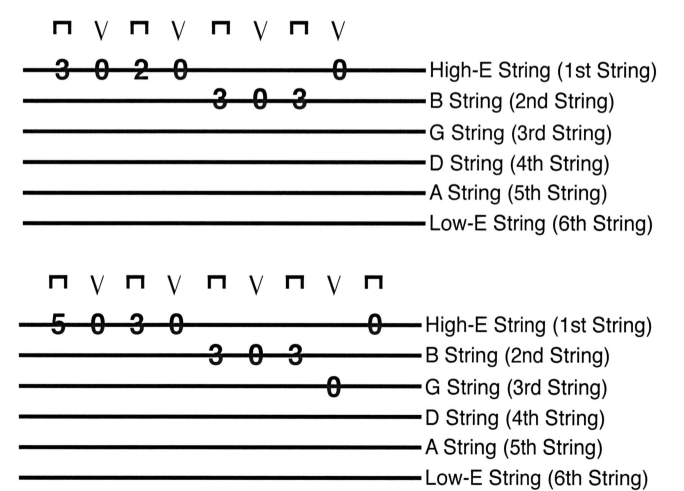

Lesson 45: Chapter 2 Overview
What We Have Learned

- Tablature Basics

- Alternate Picking

- Major Chords: Open Position C, F & E

- Strumming Techniques with Open Chords

- What are Intervals, Part 1

- What are Intervals, Part 2

- Minor Chords: Open Position A & D

- *House of the Rising Sun*

- Rock Technique: Slides

- Guitar Licks that use Slide Techniques

- Minor Chords: Open Position E & B

- Minor Chords: C, F & G

- Music Theory: Major & Minor Chords

- Pickups & Toggle Switches

- Music Theory: Learning the First-String Notes

- Power Chords

- *House of the Rising Sun:* Power-Chord Version

- Changing the Guitar Strings

- Rock Songs that use Minor Chords

- Guitar Licks Inspired by Angus Young

CHAPTER THREE: BLUES ROCK BASICS

Lesson 46:
Blues Guitar Basics

From Eric Clapton to Greg Allman to Jimi Hendrix to Stevie Ray Vaughan to Bonnie Raitt, so many great Rock guitarists have been inspired by the Blues.

In this chapter, we are going to look at Blues techniques, licks, chords, and progressions that will add some style and spice to your playing. These techniques and ideas are the starting points for a course of nearly endless musical discovery. So, take your time with this material and have fun.

As we have mentioned before in this book, part of becoming a good Rock guitarist is discovering your own musical voice. One way to grow this way, as a musician, is to look for different ways to play the materials presented in this book. Try changing the angle of your guitar pick or pluck the notes in different sections of the string. You will hear how these little variations create a considerably different sound on your instrument.

On the next page, we are going to look at our first Dominant 7th chords. These are chords that are frequently used in Rock, Blues, Jazz, Country and many other styles of music. They are similar to major chords, but have one extra note, which is called a "seventh". In technical terms, the seventh of a Dominant 7th chord is a Minor 7th interval above the Root note of the chord. (If you don't remember what an interval is, check out the lessons on intervals from chapter two of the book.)

For an A Dominant Seventh chord, the note "A" is the Root and the note "G" is the 7th of the chord (the note that is a Minor 7th interval above the Root note "A"). For a D Dominant Seventh chord, the note "D" is the Root and the note "C" is the 7th of the chord (the note that is a Minor 7th interval above the Root note "D"). Finally, for an E Dominant Seventh chord, the note "E" is the Root and the note "D" is the 7th of the chord (the note that is a Minor 7th interval above the Root note "E").

Dominant Seventh chords are abbreviated by using the letter name of the chord and the number seven. For example an A Dominant Seventh chord would be abbreviated this way: A7. An E Dominant Seventh chord would be abbreviated this way: E7.

In the chart below, you will find depictions of the A7, D7, and E7 chords. The letter names of the notes of the chords and their interval positioning are included in the diagram.

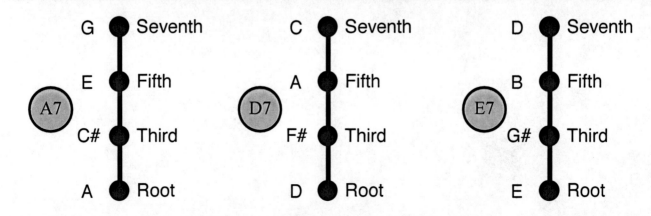

A7			D7			E7		
G	Seventh		C	Seventh		D	Seventh	
E	Fifth		A	Fifth		B	Fifth	
C#	Third		F#	Third		G#	Third	
A	Root		D	Root		E	Root	

Lesson 47: Blues Rock Dominant 7th Chords, Part 1

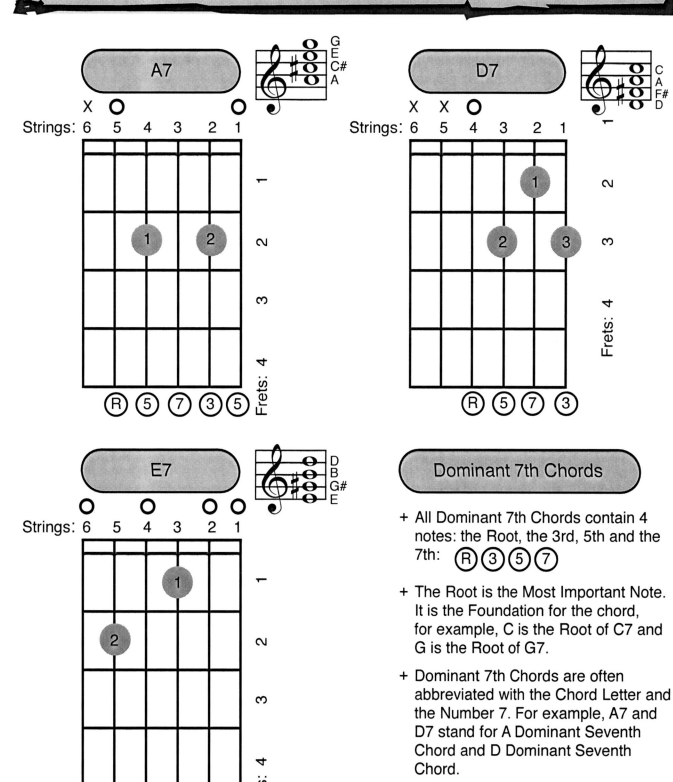

A7

Strings: 6 5 4 3 2 1

Frets: 1 2 3 4

(R) (5) (7) (3) (5)

D7

Strings: 6 5 4 3 2 1

Frets: 2 3 4

(R) (5) (7) (3)

E7

Strings: 6 5 4 3 2 1

Frets: 1 2 3 4

(R) (5) (7) (3) (5) (R)

Dominant 7th Chords

+ All Dominant 7th Chords contain 4 notes: the Root, the 3rd, 5th and the 7th: (R)(3)(5)(7)

+ The Root is the Most Important Note. It is the Foundation for the chord, for example, C is the Root of C7 and G is the Root of G7.

+ Dominant 7th Chords are often abbreviated with the Chord Letter and the Number 7. For example, A7 and D7 stand for A Dominant Seventh Chord and D Dominant Seventh Chord.

+ Dominant 7th Chords have a "bluesy" quality and can "spice" up Major Chords.

Lesson 48: Music Theory
What are Chord Progressions?

In all major and minor scales, we give the notes numbers based on their position. These numbers go from one to seven. In music, we call these numbers "scale degrees". The numbers are often written as Roman Numerals (see chart below).

The root (the main note of the scale) is always number (or degree) one. In the key of C, which is the white keys of the piano, the notes are C, D, E, F, G, A, and B. Each one of these notes is given a number from 1 to 7. Basically, the numbers just start from the root note, which is number one, and go up in order to seven. So, it's pretty simple and doesn't require any advanced math skills.

Here are the Notes and Corresponding Numbers for the Scale Degrees in the Key of C Major. The Roman Numerals for Each Scale Degree are written on the Right.

C = 1 = I
D = 2 = II
E = 3 = III
F = 4 = IV
G = 5 = V
A = 6 = VI
B = 7 = VII

A chord progression is just a fancy term that means a group of chords that follows a particular pattern. These patterns often repeat several times during a song. In Rock, Blues, Country, Metal, Folk, and Pop there are several chord progressions that are very common. You have probably heard these progressions hundreds of times.

Chord progressions are given names based on the scale degree numbers of the root notes of the chords. For instance, a chord progression in C Major that features only the chords C, F, and G is called a I, IV, V progression--pronounced like this: a one, four, five progression. Refer to the chart above and on the right for the scale degrees.

Below is a graphic representation of the scale degrees in C Major. The scale degrees are written as Roman Numerals at the bottom of the diagram.

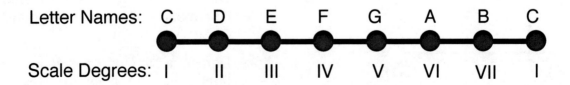

Letter Names:	C	D	E	F	G	A	B	C
Scale Degrees:	I	II	III	IV	V	VI	VII	I

Lesson 49: Twelve-Bar Blues In the Key of A

In A *12-Bar Blues*

Chord: A7	A7	A7	A7
Strum: 1 2 3 4	1 2 3 4	1 2 3 4	1 2 3 4

Chord: D7	D7	A7	A7
Strum: 1 2 3 4	1 2 3 4	1 2 3 4	1 2 3 4

Chord: E7	D7	A7	A7
Strum: 1 2 3 4	1 2 3 4	1 2 3 4	1 2 3 4

Twelve-Bar Blues

In music the word "bar" means "measure". Many Blues, Rock, and Jazz songs use a twelve-measure (or "12-Bar") format. For this format, you play the 12 measures and then return to the beginning and repeat them again. So, as you play music with family and friends, you might hear some of them use the expression "Twelve-Bar Blues" and you will know what they mean. Some famous examples of Twelve-Bar Blues are *Crossroads* by Eric Clapton and *Pride and Joy* by Stevie Ray Vaughan.

CHECK OUT VIDEO 14

Most Twelve-Bar Blues follow a I, IV, V progression (that is, a "one, four, five progression"). The Twelve-Bar Blues song in this lesson is in the key of A. So, the A7 chord is the I chord ("the one chord"). The D7 chord is the IV chord ("the four chord"). The E7 chord is the V chord ("the five chord"). Once you learn this song, try it out with the Play-Along Video.

After you have played through the "12-Bar Blues" a few times with 4 strums per measure, try experimenting with different strumming patterns and rhythms. ***Have Fun!***

Lesson 50: Rockabilly Groove, Overview

Rockabilly is a mix of Blues, Rock, Jazz and Country. It was popularized in the 1950s by artists like Elvis and Chuck Berry. Two good examples of the style are *Hound Dog* by Elvis and *Johnny Be Good* by Chuck Berry. Take a few minutes today and check out recordings of these songs on Youtube. You might also like to hear *Rock This Town* by the Stray Cats.

CHECK OUT VIDEO 15

Our Rockabilly Lessons (on the next few pages) involve chord patterns played on only 2 adjacent strings. When playing these lessons, try to isolate each 2-string chord and make short strums with your Right Hand. Check out the video lesson to see and hear how this technique works.

The example below shows the basic pattern. For this example, only play the 5th and 4th strings (the A & D strings). Use your index finger (1st finger) for the notes on the second fret. For notes on the fourth fret, try to use your ring finger (3rd finger). If this is too much of a stretch, try using your pinky (4th finger) to play the notes on the fourth fret.

For the Rockabilly material on the next few pages, take your time and master each two-string pattern. Then, slowly try linking them together. First try linking the A Riff and the D Riff.

All Down Strums for the Pattern

```
————————————————————————————————— High-E String (1st String)
————————————————————————————————— B String (2nd String)
————————————————————————————————— G String (3rd String)
—2——2——4——4——2——2——4——4————————— D String (4th String)
—0——0——0——0——0——0——0——0————————— A String (5th String)
————————————————————————————————— Low-E String (6th String)
```

Play all of these notes on the 4th & 5th Strings.

Lesson 51: Rockabilly Groove, Part 1: In the Key of A

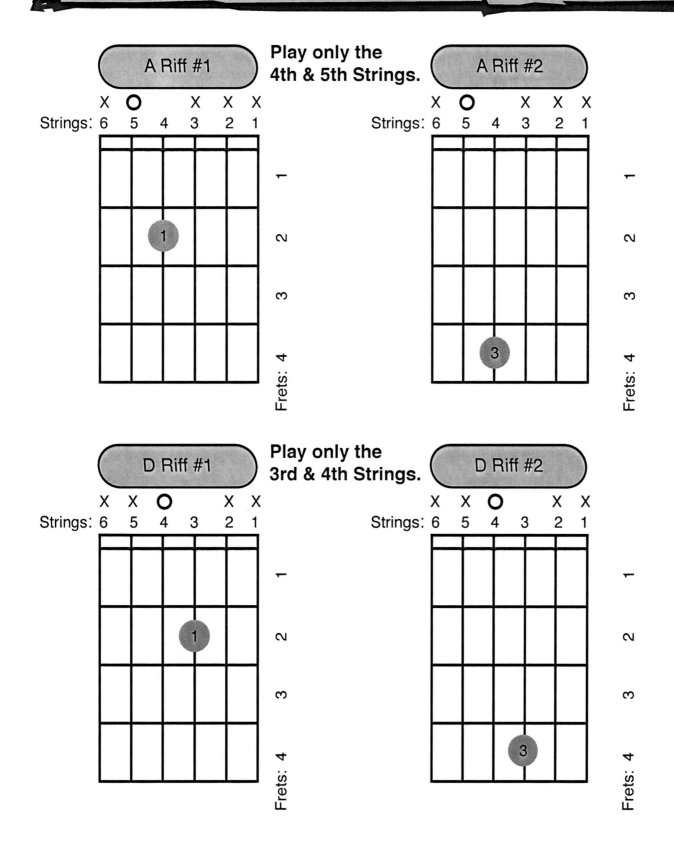

A Riff #1

Play only the 4th & 5th Strings.

A Riff #2

D Riff #1

Play only the 3rd & 4th Strings.

D Riff #2

Lesson 52: Rockabilly Groove & Song
Part 2: In the Key of A

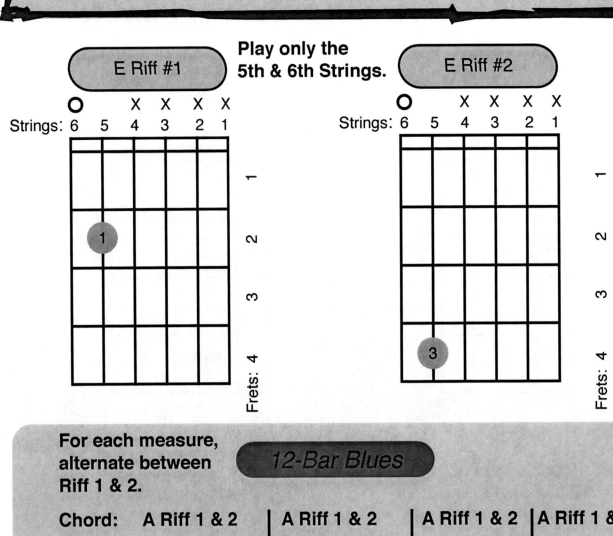

E Riff #1

Play only the 5th & 6th Strings.

E Riff #2

Strings: 6 5 4 3 2 1

1

Fret: 1 2 3 4

Strings: 6 5 4 3 2 1

3

Fret: 1 2 3 4

For each measure, alternate between Riff 1 & 2.

12-Bar Blues

Chord:	A Riff 1 & 2	A Riff 1 & 2	A Riff 1 & 2	A Riff 1 & 2
Strum:	1 2 3 4	1 2 3 4	1 2 3 4	1 2 3 4
Chord:	D Riff 1 & 2	D Riff 1 & 2	A Riff 1 & 2	A Riff 1 & 2
Strum:	1 2 3 4	1 2 3 4	1 2 3 4	1 2 3 4
Chord:	E Riff 1 & 2	D Riff 1 & 2	A Riff 1 & 2	A Riff 1 & 2
Strum:	1 2 3 4	1 2 3 4	1 2 3 4	1 2 3 4

Lesson 53:
Rock Technique: Vibrato

Vibrato is one of the most expressive techniques in guitar playing. The technique, which involves slightly moving the guitar string up and down or side to side, will give the sound of the notes you play a shimmering, vocal quality. When you add vibrato to your playing, you will emulate the techniques of Rock, Blues, and Jazz singers on your guitar. This will make the musical phrases that you play sound more expressive and dramatic.

We will be looking at two types of vibrato: Wide Vibrato and Close Vibrato. Check out the video lesson to learn more information.

**CHECK OUT
VIDEO 16**

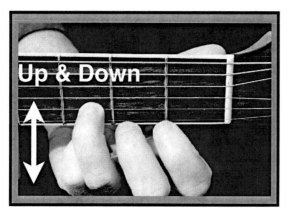

For a more intense vibrato, wiggle your finger up and down, while pressing down on the string.

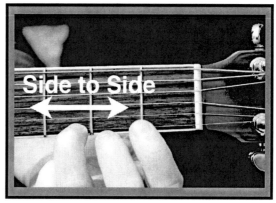

For a more subtle vibrato, wiggle your finger side to side, while pressing down on the string.

To create a wide, dramatic vibrato, place the left-hand third finger on a fret (let's try the 3rd fret of the B string) and move your finger in an up-and-down motion, after plucking the B string. Listen to sound quality. If you need more support for your third finger, you might want to place your first and second fingers on the first and second frets of the B string, respectively. This will provide greater leverage on the string. Once you have this technique down, try to vary the speed of your up-and-down movements. The faster your vibrato, the more energy and wildness will be in the sound.

For a more subtle vibrato, fret a note with your left hand and wiggle your finger back and forth after plucking the string. This is a great sounding vibrato for ballads and slow songs. Listen to Eric Clapton and Jimi Hendrix for vibrato styles.

Lesson 54: Vibrato Licks

Here are three guitar licks that use vibrato. Try varying the speed of your vibrato, as well as using vibrato with both the up-and-down motion and the side-to-side motion. Listen to the difference in the sound with each version.

〰〰 This symbol, above the tablature staff, indicates to use vibrato on a note. The symbol does not indicate the speed of the vibrato; that is up to you.

**CHECK OUT
VIDEO 17**

1.

〰〰

```
High-E String (1st String)
---0---3------------------- B String (2nd String)
--------2---0----2---0----- G String (3rd String)
----------------------2---- D String (4th String)
--------------------------- A String (5th String)
--------------------------- Low-E String (6th String)
```

2.

〰〰

```
--------------------------- High-E String (1st String)
----------------3---0------ B String (2nd String)
----------0---2--------2--- G String (3rd String)
---0---2------------------- D String (4th String)
--------------------------- A String (5th String)
--------------------------- Low-E String (6th String)
```

3.

〰〰

```
---3---0------------------- High-E String (1st String)
----------3---0------------ B String (2nd String)
----------------2---0---2-- G String (3rd String)
--------------------------- D String (4th String)
--------------------------- A String (5th String)
--------------------------- Low-E String (6th String)
```

You can play all of the vibrato licks in this chapter over *Undertow Blues,* which can be found later in this chapter.

Lesson 55: More Vibrato Licks

Here are four more guitar licks that use vibrato. You can use all of the vibrato licks from this page and the previous page to make a guitar solo in *Undertow Blues,* which is featured a little later in this book and videos.

**CHECK OUT
VIDEO 17**

1.
~~~ ~~~ ~~ ~~

								High-E String (1st String)
								B String (2nd String)
2	2	2	2	0				G String (3rd String)
					2	2	0	2	D String (4th String)
								A String (5th String)
								Low-E String (6th String)

2.
~~~

3	3	0	3	3	0	3	High-E String (1st String)
							B String (2nd String)
							G String (3rd String)
							D String (4th String)
							A String (5th String)
							Low-E String (6th String)

3.
~~~

						High-E String (1st String)
						B String (2nd String)
						G String (3rd String)
0	2		0	2		2	D String (4th String)
		0	2		0	2	A String (5th String)
						Low-E String (6th String)

4.
~~~

							High-E String (1st String)
							B String (2nd String)
				2	0		G String (3rd String)
			0	2		2	D String (4th String)
	0	2					A String (5th String)
0	3						Low-E String (6th String)

Lesson 56: Secret to Guitar Success #6: Listen to Music Outside Your Comfort Zone

This week, as you work on improving your guitar playing and musicianship, have a little fun by listening to some genres and styles of music outside of your regular listening comfort zone. The best musicians often have a broad knowledge of music and can draw inspiration from many styles.

By exposing yourself to new artists and genres you will grow in new and unexpected ways as a guitarist. For instance, if you are a Blues fan and try listening to a few Classical recordings, you might get some new ideas for sound colors and textures on the electric guitar. If you are a Metal player and listen to some Jazz recordings, you might get some new ideas for riffs and rhythms.

Online there are a number of streaming music services that offer a free version. Spotify and Pandora are the most popular at the moment. You might also do some genre searches on Youtube. *Have Fun!*

Lesson 57: Secret to Guitar Success #7: Listen to Yourself

Every few days or once a week, record yourself playing some of your favorite songs or licks. You don't need to have an expensive recording device. If you have a microphone and some dictation or recording software on your phone, tablet or computer, those will work as well.

These recordings do not need to be high fidelity. The purpose of recording yourself is to listen to your playing from an "outside" perspective. When you press the playback, pay attention to your rhythm, the evenness of your tone and playing, and your expression. Every week, try to make slight improvements in these areas.

Have a positive and constructive attitude when you are listening to these recordings. Try not to get hung up on small details or little mistakes. Instead, listen to any awkward patterns or habits in your playing and work on improving in those areas.

As a side benefit, this practice will also get you used to the process of recording. So, if you are ever in a recording studio or at a friend's house making a recording, the process will not feel that unusual to you. You will be right at home.

Lesson 58: A Word about Scales & the Blues Scale

- Scales are groups of notes arranged in stepwise patterns, either going up or down. The combination of these steps (also called "intervals") gives each type of scale its unique sound and character.
- On this page, we are going to start learning about the Blues Scale: one of the most popular scales that is used in Rock Music. **Have Fun!**

String
Name: E A D G B E
Number: 6 5 4 3 2 1 Fret:

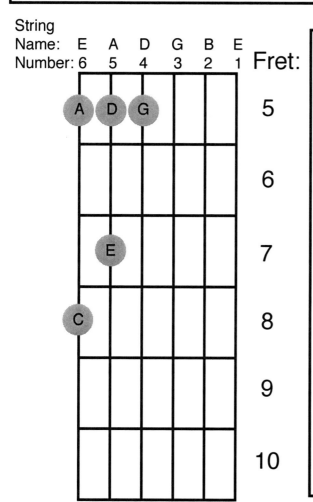

Fret:
5
6
7
8
9
10

- The Blues Scale (also called "Pentatonic Minor") is a 5-Note Scale that is used in Rock, Jazz, Pop, Country, and Blues songs.
- Take a look at the chart on the left. It displays the 5 notes of the Blues Scale in the key of A. In the key of A, the notes are A, C, D, E, and G.
- On your guitar, locate the 5th fret of the 6th String (the Low E String or thickest string). Play the notes of the scale pattern from the chart on the left and listen to the character of the sound.
- Below, you will find a chart that displays the notes of the Blues Scale in standard notation (with letter names included.
- In the next few pages, we will be learning more about the Blues Scale.

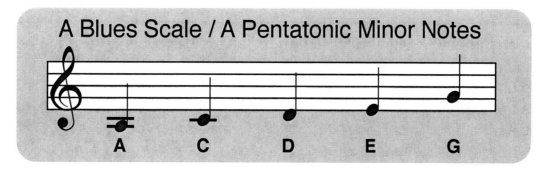

A Blues Scale / A Pentatonic Minor Notes

A   C   D   E   G

Lesson 59: The Blues Scale in E: Using Open Strings

The first blues scale form that we are going to learn is the Blues Scale in E. This form of the blues scale uses one open-string note and one fretted note on each string. So, it is the easiest form to play. On the Low-E, High-E, and B strings you will use your second finger (Middle Finger) to play the notes on the 3rd fret. For the other strings (the A, D, and G strings), you will use the first finger (Index Finger) to play the notes on the 2nd fret.

The E Blues Scale contains the following notes from low to high: E, G, A, B, and D. In the chart below, this group of notes repeats and an additional note (a "G") is added. The notes for the E Blues Scale in the chart below are the following (from low to high): E, G, A, B, D, E, G, A, B, D, E, and G.

The blues scale is a very versatile improvisation tool for Rock music. You can use it to play guitar solos, create riffs and licks, and add embellishments to your playing. Around 80-90% of all Rock guitar solos use some form of the blues scale.

In the chart below, you will find the fingerings for the E Blues Scale. Take some time to play through this scale pattern going from the lowest string (the Low-E string) to the highest string (the High-E string). Memorize the notes and finger patterns.

If you are curious to learn more about scales and licks using scales, check out *Guitar Scales Handbook*, also by Damon Ferrante.

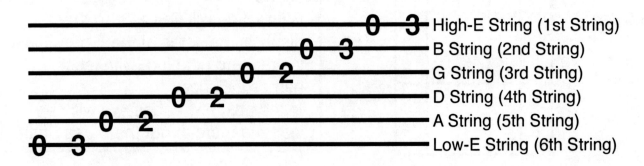

Notes on the Low-E String (6th String): "E" on the Open String / "G" on the 3rd Fret
Notes on A String (5th String): "A" on the Open String / "B" on the 2nd Fret
Notes on D String (4th String): "D" on the Open String / "E" on the 2nd Fret
Notes on G String (3rd String): "G" on the Open String / "A" on the 2nd Fret
Notes on B String (2nd String): "B" on the Open String / "D" on the 3rd Fret
Notes on High-E String (1st String): "E" on the Open String / "G" on the 3rd Fret

Lesson 60: The Blues Licks in E: Using Open Strings

Here are four guitar licks that use open strings in the E Blues Scale. Try them one at a time using finger number one of your left hand.

CHECK OUT VIDEO 18

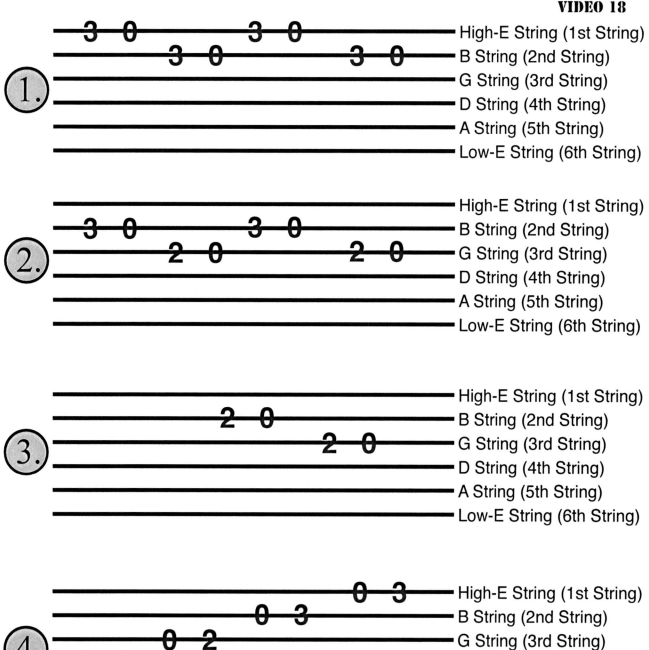

Lesson 61: The Blues Licks in E: Using Open Strings & Slides

Here are four guitar licks that use slides and open strings in the E Blues Scale. Try them one at a time using finger number one of your left hand. Then, once you have mastered them, try playing them in order from number four to number one. In other words, play 4, 3, 2, 1, as one big combination guitar lick.

CHECK OUT
VIDEO 18

1.
```
2-3 0    2-3 0 ———— High-E String (1st String)
    3 0        3 0 ——— B String (2nd String)
————————————————————— G String (3rd String)
————————————————————— D String (4th String)
————————————————————— A String (5th String)
————————————————————— Low-E String (6th String)
```

2.
```
————————————————————— High-E String (1st String)
2-3 0    2-3 0 ———— B String (2nd String)
    2 0        2 0 — G String (3rd String)
————————————————————— D String (4th String)
————————————————————— A String (5th String)
————————————————————— Low-E String (6th String)
```

3.
```
————————————————————— High-E String (1st String)
————————————————————— B String (2nd String)
1-2 0    1-2 0 ———— G String (3rd String)
    2 0        2 0 — D String (4th String)
————————————————————— A String (5th String)
————————————————————— Low-E String (6th String)
```

4.
```
                  2-3 0 — High-E String (1st String)
            2-3 0 ———— B String (2nd String)
    0 2 ——————————————— G String (3rd String)
0 2 ——————————————————— D String (4th String)
————————————————————— A String (5th String)
————————————————————— Low-E String (6th String)
```

Lesson 62: Blues Licks in E: Using Open Strings & Bass Notes

Here are four guitar licks that use lower notes and open strings in the E Blues Scale. Try them one at a time using finger number one of your left hand.

CHECK OUT
VIDEO 18

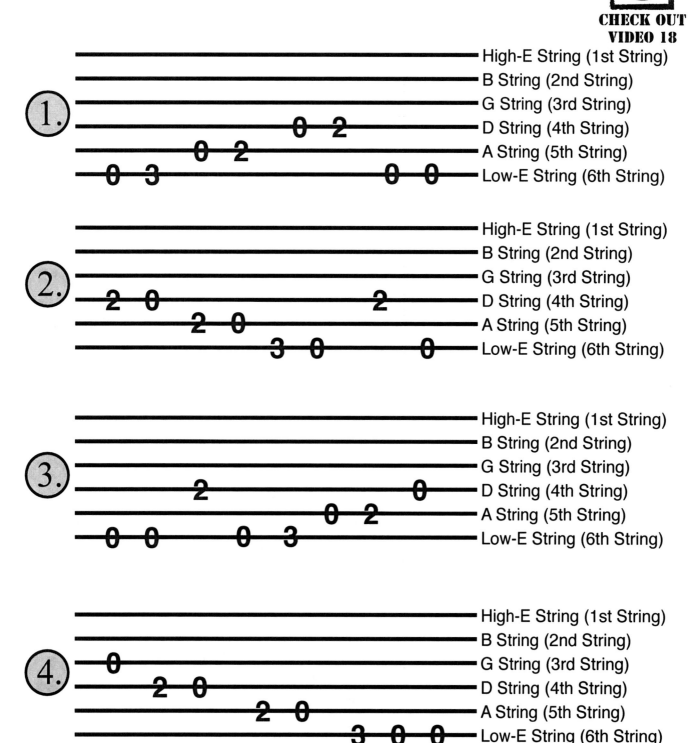

Lesson 63: Blues Licks with Slides and Vibrato

Here are four more guitar licks that use vibrato. You can use all of the vibrato licks from this page and the previous page to make a guitar solo in *Undertow Blues,* which is featured a little later in this book and videos.

CHECK OUT VIDEO 18

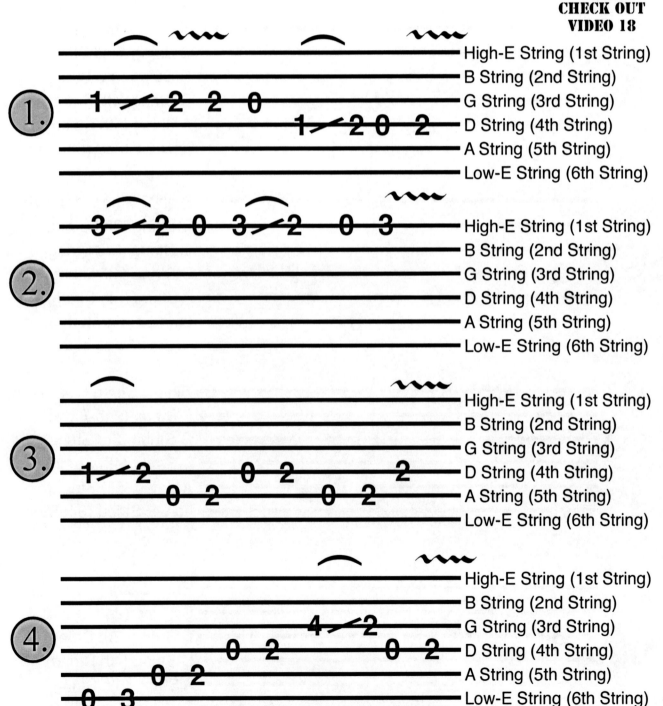

Lesson 64: Dominant 7th Chords Open Position

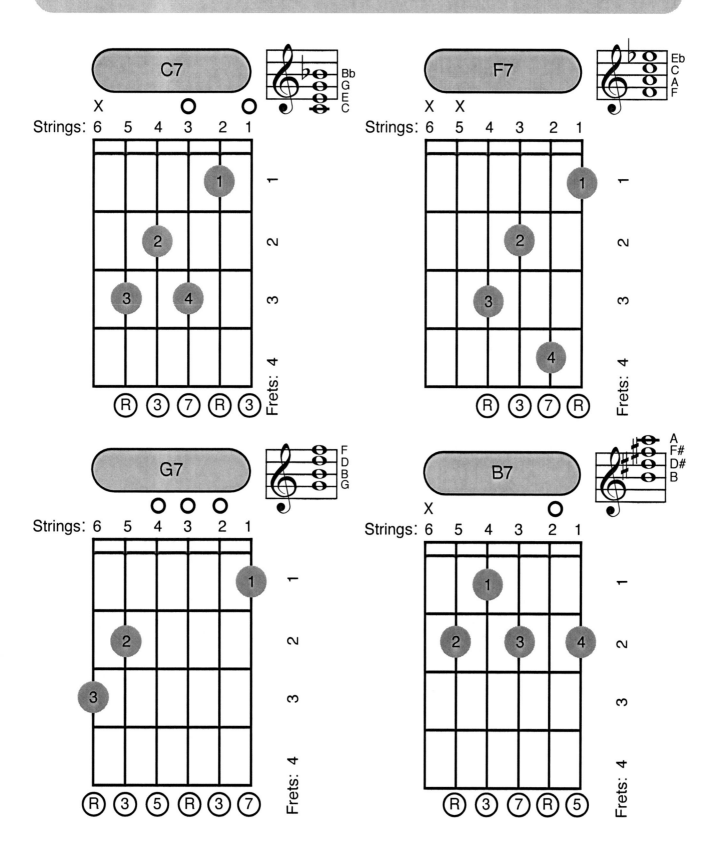

Lesson 65: *Undertow Blues*

Twelve-Bar Blues

In *Undertow Blues*, you will be playing the E7, A7, and B7 chords. If you do not remember the fingerings of these chords, you will need to refer back to some of the earlier lessons in this chapter (where you will find the positions). The B7 chord takes a little bit of coordination. So, before you strum through this song, try alternating between the A7 and B7 chords ten times in a row. Then play B7, A7, and E7 in succession.

After you have played through this song a few times in the video lesson, try making a guitar solo over the Play-Along video using the open-string and vibrato guitar licks in E that you have learned in the last few lessons. Also try creating slight variations on these guitar licks by repeating notes, changing the rhythms, and adding new notes.

Have Fun!

CHECK OUT VIDEO 19

In E

Undertow Blues

Chord:	E7	E7	E7	E7
Strum:	1 2 3 4	1 2 3 4	1 2 3 4	1 2 3 4

Chord:	A7	A7	E7	E7
Strum:	1 2 3 4	1 2 3 4	1 2 3 4	1 2 3 4

Chord:	B7	A7	E7	E7
Strum:	1 2 3 4	1 2 3 4	1 2 3 4	1 2 3 4

Lesson 66: Music Theory Learning the Second String Notes

The 2nd String

	Fret
Strings: 6 5 4 3 2 1	
C	1
Also Db — C#	2
D	3
Also Eb — D#	4
E	5
F	6
Also Gb — F#	7
G	8
Also Ab — G#	9
A	10
Also A# — Bb	11

Great job with your guitar playing! You are making a lot of progress. Now, it's time to start learning the notes on the 2nd string (the B string) of the fretboard. This is a very important skill to have as a guitarist. So, let's get to work learning these note names.

The note "B" is the open string.

1. Find the note "C" on your guitar and play it. Check the chart on the left to see if you are on the right fret.
2. Find the note "D" on your guitar and play it. Check the chart on the left to see if you are on the right fret.
3. Find the note "F" on your guitar and play it. Check the chart on the left to see if you are on the right fret.
4. Find the note "E" on your guitar and play it. Check the chart on the left to see if you are on the right fret.
5. Find the note "G" on your guitar and play it. Check the chart on the left to see if you are on the right fret.
6. Find the note "A" on your guitar and play it. Check the chart on the left to see if you are on the right fret.
7. Find the note "C#" on your guitar and play it. Check the chart on the left to see if you are on the right fret.

Repeat this exercise each day, using all of the notes listed in the chart on the left, until you can find the notes with ease.

If you are not 100% sure of the notes on the High-E string (the 1st string), take a moment now and go over the note-naming exercises from Chapter Two. As you learn these notes, you will be greatly improving your understanding of the layout of the guitar, making you a better musician.

Lesson 67: Licks Inspired by Great Rock Guitarists: Eric Clapton

Here are two exercises to improve your slide and vibrato technique. Repeat each exercise at a comfortable tempo for between 1 and 2 minutes. If your hand or wrist starts to feel tired, just shake it out and take a break for a while. Never practice to the point of discomfort or pain. If you feel any discomfort or pain while playing, that is your body's way of telling you it's time to put the guitar down and take a break for awhile.

**CHECK OUT
VIDEO 20**

Eric Clapton is one of the world's great Rock guitarists. Among his many stylistic trademarks are his use of string bending, vibrato, tasteful blues lines, rhythmic grooves, and slides. You might check out some of the songs that feature these elements of Eric Clapton's playing: *Layla, Tears in Heaven, Crossroads,* and *Sunshine of Your Love.*

These two licks are based on something Eric Clapton might play over a bluesy Rock song like *Layla.* They involve slide and vibrato and primarily use the second and third strings (the B string and G string, respectively). They work well over an E7 Chord or if you are playing a Blues / Rock song in the key of E. You can try these two licks to create a guitar solo in *Undertow Blues. **Have Fun!***

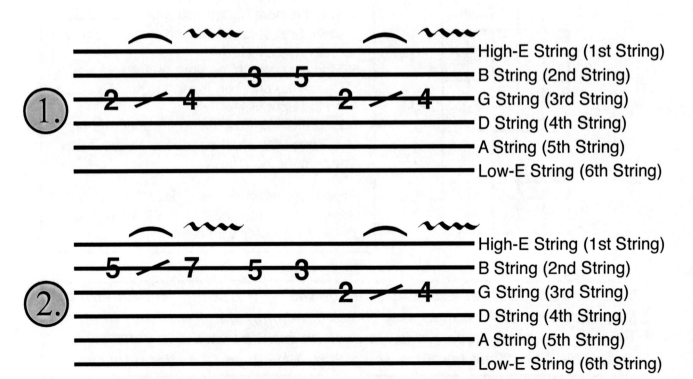

Lesson 68: Check Out These Songs that Use Blues Techniques

Take a little time now and listen to the following rock songs that use Blues techniques and chords. You might check out Youtube or the artists' websites for free recordings and performance videos. Listen to the guitar parts in each song and try to pick up ideas and sounds for licks, solos, and, chords, which you can then add your own playing. Take a moment and listen to these songs in an active way, focusing on the guitar sound for each artist.

Here are a few:

• Stevie Ray Vaughan: *Texas Flood*

• Eric Clapton: *Layla*

• B.B. King: *The Thrill is Gone*

• Jimi Hendrix: *Voodoo Chile*

• Stray Cats: *Stray Cat Strut*

• Danny Gatton: *Blues Newburg*

• Dire Straits: *Money for Nothing*

• Eric Johnson: *S.R.V*

• Led Zeppelin: *Rock and Roll*

Lesson 69: Chapter 3 Overview
What We Have Learned

Take a little time to go back over some of the concepts from this chapter's lessons. If there was an element that you are not sure about spend a day or two and go back over the lesson. If there is a corresponding video, check that out as well.

- Blues Guitar Basics

- Dominant 7th Chords

- Music Theory: What are Chord Progressions?

- Twelve-Bar Blues

- Rockabilly Overview

- Rockabilly Riffs

- Rock Technique: Vibrato

- Vibrato Licks

- Music Theory: What is the Blues Scale?

- Rock Technique: The Blues Scale in E

- Blues Scale Licks Using Open Strings

- *Undertow Blues*

- Music Theory: Notes of the Second String

- Licks Inspired by Great Guitarists: Eric Clapton

- Songs That Use Blues Techniques

CHAPTER FOUR: RHYTHM GUITAR

Rhythm Guitar Overview

Strumming Patterns

Palm Muting

Funk Chords

Barre Chords

Rockabilly Bass Lines

Arpeggiated Chords

Great Rock Guitarists

Chapter Review

Lesson 70: Rhythm Guitar Overview

In this chapter, we are going to look at some beginning concepts in rhythm guitar playing. Each of these lessons is the starting point for you to explore broader concepts. Good rhythm guitar playing is a vital part of Rock music. It not only helps create the groove of the music, but you will also help to tell the story of a song by the way you play the chords and riffs.

The rhythm guitar techniques that are covered here will spice up your playing. The first lesson goes over four common strumming patterns used in Rock. You can apply most of these patterns in various sections of any Rock song to add a little variety to the sound. Next, we will look at palm muting. This is a technique that can greatly change the color of your sound. We will also look at Funk and Reggae styles in a lesson. Near the end of the chapter, we will go over barre chords; these are moveable chords, which will allow you to play songs in any key. Barre chords require a little bit of finger strength. In the last few lessons of the chapter, we will explore how to use arpeggio techniques (playing one note of a chord at a time) to create chord textures and Rockabilly bass lines.

These are a few (of the many) great Rock guitarists whose rhythm guitar playing you should check out to get some inspiration for your own playing:

Jimi Hendrix: His rhythm playing grew out of Blues and Motown styles. Through his genius, he took rhythm guitar playing to a whole new level. Have a listen to *Little Wing* and *All Along the Watchtower*.

Keith Richards: The great rhythm guitarist of the Rolling Stones, Keith Richards has created a distinctive Rock sound that uses power chords and added chord tones. Have a listen to the Rolling Stones' *Beast of Burden, Jumpin' Jack Flash,* and *Start Me Up.*

John Frusciante: His very sensitive approach to rhythm, where he explores the range of the guitar and also leaves room for silences, can be an inspiration for all Rock guitarists. Take a listen to his great Funk-inspired playing on the Red Hot Chili Peppers' *Under the Bridge, Around the World,* and *By the Way.*

Before we get started with the rhythm guitar ideas in this chapter, try this simple, but effective technique. Play some of your favorite chords by strumming near the bridge of your guitar. Listen to the quality of the sound; it should be a little bit metallic in tone. Now, try strumming the same chords near the neck of your guitar; these should sound warmer and fuller. You can create great effects by just strumming your chords in different places along the neck. Have fun exploring this!

Lesson 71: Basic Rock Guitar Strumming Patterns

Here are four examples of basic Rock guitar strumming patterns. All of the examples are in 4/4 time; so, you should count "1 & 2 & 3 & 4 &" for each measure. The "&" (or "and") stands for the upbeat (the halfway point for each beat). The down arrows represent down strums and the up arrows represent up strums.

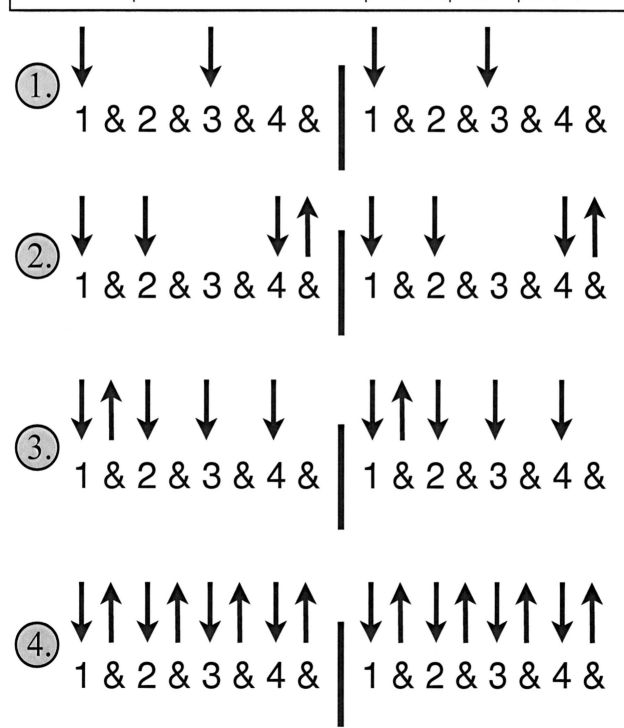

Lesson 72: Rock Technique Palm Muting

Palm Muting

• As you strum these chords, try gently placing your right-hand palm on top of the strings. This will dampen the sound and change its character.

• Try strumming the power chords in the first line <u>without</u> palm muting and in the second line <u>with</u> palm muting.

• Try strumming beats 1 and 2 (the first two beats of each measure) with palm muting. Then, lift your right hand up and play beats 3 and 4 (the last two beats of each measure) without palm muting.

• Experiment with different combinations of palm muting.

Index Finger on the 3rd Fret		Rock in C		

Chord:	C5	C5	G5	G5
Strum:	1 2 3 4	1 2 3 4	1 2 3 4	1 2 3 4

Chord:	C5	C5	G5	G5
Strum:	1 2 3 4	1 2 3 4	1 2 3 4	1 2 3 4

Lesson 73: Funk & Reggae-Style Chords

- To create a Funk-Style strumming pattern, strum an up / down pattern twice, very fast.
- Then, pause (rest) for four beats and strum the pattern again.

- To create a Reggae-Style strumming pattern, palm mute the 1st & 3rd beats and do up-strums on the 2nd and 4th beats.
- M = Mute
- ↑ = Up-strum pattern

Funk-Style Chords

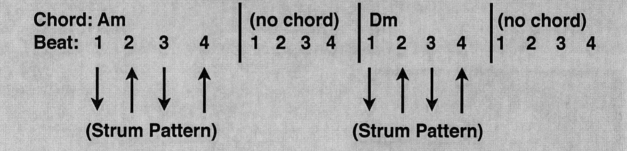

Chord: Am	(no chord)	Dm	(no chord)
Beat: 1 2 3 4	1 2 3 4	1 2 3 4	1 2 3 4

(Strum Pattern)   (Strum Pattern)

Reggae-Style Chords

Chord: Em	Am	Em	Am
Beat: 1 2 3 4	1 2 3 4	1 2 3 4	1 2 3 4
M ↑ M ↑	M ↑ M ↑	M ↑ M ↑	M ↑ M ↑

Lesson 74: Secret to Guitar Success #8: Keep an Open Mind

Each day, try to draw inspiration for your guitar playing from the world around you. It might be things as varied as the combinations of sounds from many simultaneous conversations that you hear at a cafeteria or the rhythmic, cloud-like motion of flock of birds. Metaphorically speaking, keep your eyes and ears open to the things happening around you. You never know what small thing might turn into a big inspiration.

Lesson 75: Secret to Guitar Success #9: From Time to Time, Try New Gear

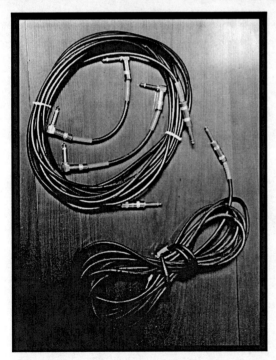

From time to time, you should try out new gear on your guitar. For the most part, this will entail changing things that are not expensive. For instance, you might try using a thinner or thicker guitar pick. Just by making this small modification to your playing, you will change the character of your sound. You might also try using a different brand or gauge ("thickness") of strings. Different brands of cables will also affect the sound of your guitar in substantial ways. Also, raising or lowering the height of your pickups will alter the tone and signal of your guitar. There should be screws near the top and bottom of each pickup that will allow you to change their height.

All of these above-mentioned examples are either free or inexpensive. So, before you decide that you need a new amp or guitar, try changing some of the elements listed above. You might be pleasantly surprised by the results.

Lesson 76: Major Barre Chords

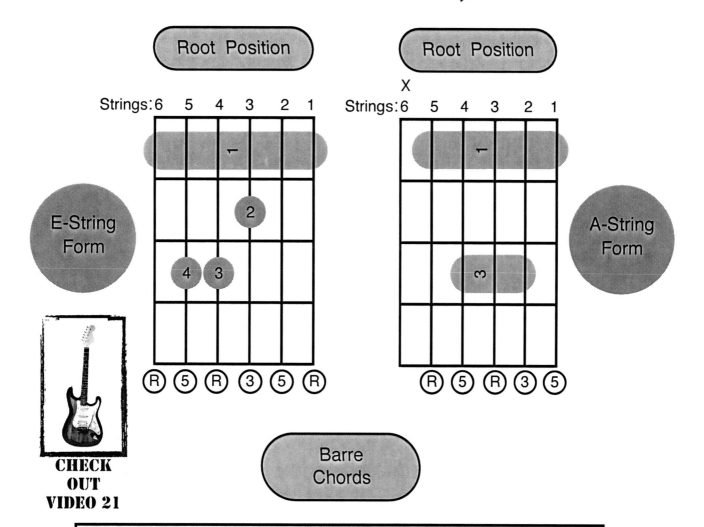

Root Position

Root Position

Strings: 6 5 4 3 2 1

Strings: 6 5 4 3 2 1

E-String Form

A-String Form

Barre Chords

CHECK OUT VIDEO 21

- For Barre Chords, the Index Finger (Finger Number 1) is placed over 5 or 6 Strings.
- These Chords are very helpful, since they are full-sounding, Moveable Chords.
- They do require a fair amount of finger strength.
- So, take your time in practicing them.
- It is best to start with the index finger "clamp" and then gradually add the notes of the chord.

Lesson 77: Minor Barre Chords

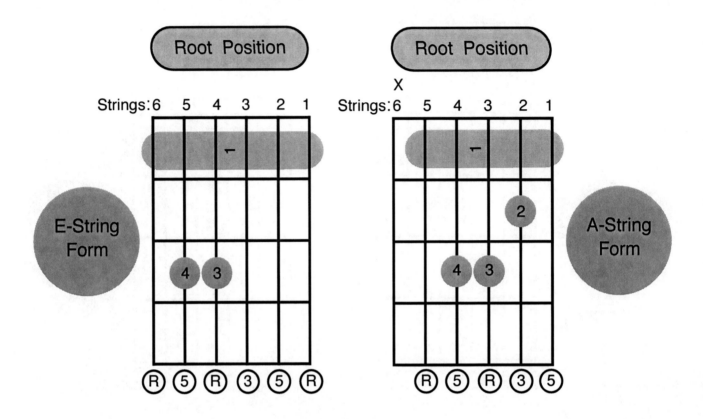

- For Minor Barre Chords, the Index Finger (Finger Number 1) is placed over 5 or 6 Strings.
- These Chords are very similar to the Major Barre Chord forms.
- The most common forms (shown above) are on the 6th and 5th Strings.
- Like the Major Barre Chord forms, they also require a bit of finger strength. So, take your time in practicing them.
- It is best to start with the index finger "clamp" and then gradually add the notes of the chord.

Lesson 78:
Dominant 7th Barre Chords

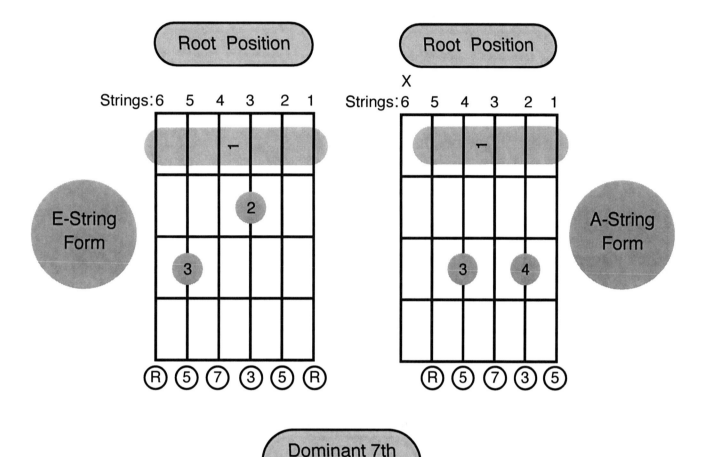

Root Position

Root Position

E-String Form

A-String Form

Dominant 7th Barre Chords

- For Dominant 7th Barre Chords, the Index Finger is placed over 5 or 6 Strings.
- These Chords are very helpful, since they are full-sounding, Moveable Chords.
- The E-String Form has a similar shape to the open E7 chord from Lesson 47.
- The A-String Form has a similar shape to the open A7 chord, also from Lesson 47.

Lesson 79: *House of the Rising Sun*
Using Barre Chords

Barre-Chord Positions for *House of the Rising Sun*

E-String Forms:

- Am: Index finger on the 5th Fret
- C : Index finger on the 8th Fret
- D : Index finger on the 10th Fret
- F : Index finger on the 1st Fret
- E : Open Position (no Barre Chord)

A-String Forms:

- Am: Open Position (no Barre Chord)
- C : Index finger on the 3rd Fret
- D : Index finger on the 5th Fret
- F : Index finger on the 8th Fret
- E : Index finger on the 7th Fret

House of the Rising Sun

Chord:	Am			C			D			F		
	There	is	a	house	in		New	Or-		leans	they	
Strum:	1	2	3	1	2	3	1	2	3	1	2	3

Chord:	Am			C			E			E		
	call	the	ris-	ing			sun.				It's	
Strum:	1	2	3	1	2	3	1	2	3	1	2	3

Chord:	Am			C			D			F		
	been	the	ruin	of			many	poor		souls	and	
Strum:	1	2	3	1	2	3	1	2	3	1	2	3

Chord:	Am			E			Am			Am		
	Lord,	I		know	I'm		one.					
Strum:	1	2	3	1	2	3	1	2	3	1	2	3

Lesson 80: Rock Technique
Arpeggiated Chords & Bass Lines

ARPEGGIATED CHORDS

An arpeggio is just a chord played one note at a time instead of strummed all at once. The word "arpeggio" comes from the Italian word for harp ("arpa"). By playing a chord and plucking each note individually, you will create a harp-like sound on the guitar. If you are curious to learn more about how to use arpeggios in your guitar playing, check out *Guitar Arpeggio Handbook*, also by Damon Ferrante.

Let's start practicing this technique by forming the C Major chord in open position. (Check out Lesson 25, if you need the chord fingering). Once you have formed the C Major chord in your left hand, pluck one string of the chord at a time, going from the 5th string to the 1st string (thickest string to thinnest string). You may either use only down strums or use alternate picking on each note. Either way is valid and will sound slightly different. So, it's good to try both methods.

Next, try arpeggiating the C Major chord by going from the 5th string (the A string) to the 1st string (the High-E string) and then going back from the 1st string to the 5th string. Try this a few times in succession, while letting each note of the chord ring out. This will create a harp-like effect. It's a great technique to add to your rhythm guitar style. Now you have arpeggiated the C Major chord. Good Job!

Try alternating between the C Major chord and the F Major chord (both found in Lesson 25) and arpeggiating the chords. For the F Major chord, you may add the open High-E string. This will create a Major Seventh chord for the F chord and will share a common tone (the "E" note) with the C Major chord.

BLUES BASS LINES

In the next few lessons, we will also look at some techniques for creating bass lines in your rhythm guitar playing. These ideas are especially useful if you want to add some variety to your accompaniment style in Blues-based Rock songs. For one verse of a song, you might want to outline the chord notes on the lower, bass strings of your guitar, rather than strumming the chords.

For these bass-line ideas, you might like to try doing some palm muting and plucking the strings in a percussive manner, like an upright or electric bass. Imagine in your mind that you are a bassist and you will get closer to the sound.

Lesson 81: Rock Ballad with Arpeggiated Chords

In this lesson you will play a 1950s Rock and Roll Ballad chord progression with arpeggiated open chords. The first chord is C Major. The second chord is A Minor. The third chord is D Minor. The final chord is G Major. Play each of these lines (one through four) and then repeat them from the beginning a few times. Try to let the notes of each chord ring out while you are playing.

CHECK OUT VIDEO 22

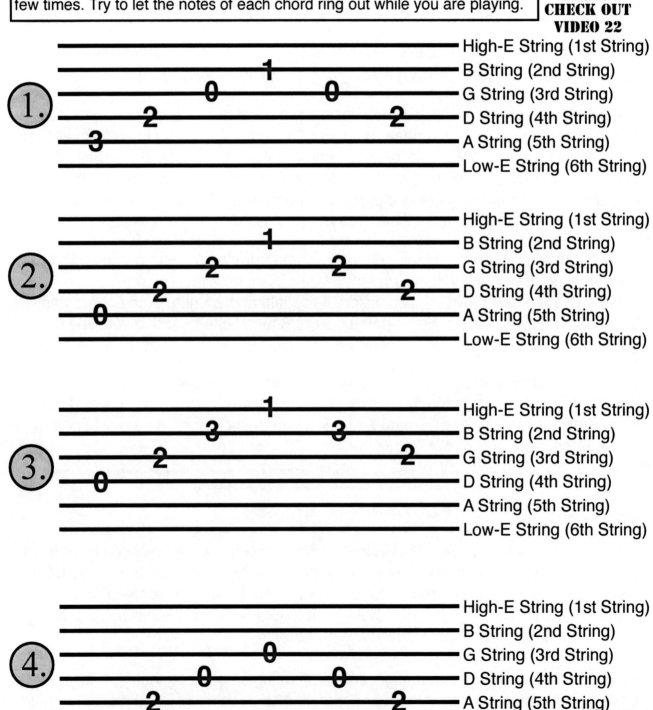

Lesson 82: Rockabilly Bass Line Part 1

In the next two lessons, we will learn how to play a walking bass line that will work over Rock, Blues, and Rockabilly. It is in the key of G. On this page, lines one and two work over a G Major or G Dominant Seventh chord. Lines three and four work over a C Major or C Dominant Seventh chord. Try playing these licks with the palm-muting technique.

CHECK OUT VIDEO 23

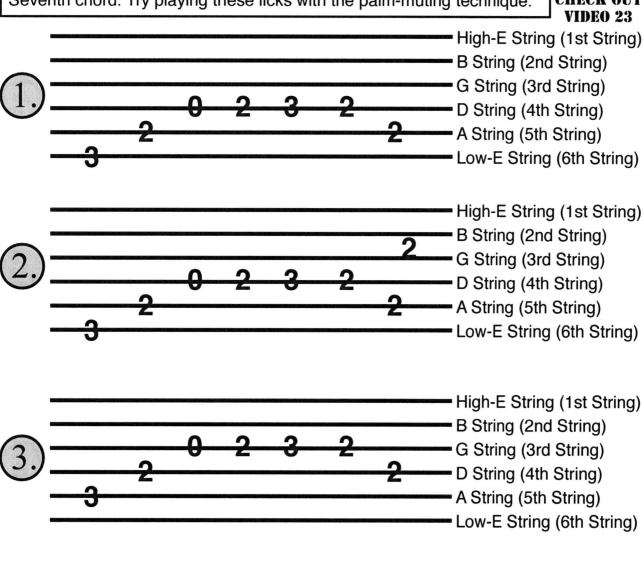

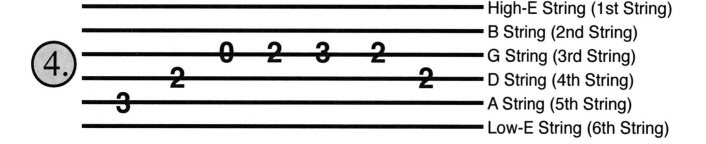

Lesson 83: Rockabilly Bass Line Part 2

This lesson continues the walking bass line idea from the previous lesson. Lines one and four work over a G Major or G Dominant Seventh chord. Line two works over a D Major or D Dominant Seventh chord. Line three works over a C Major or C Dominant Seventh chord. Once you have mastered these two lessons, put them together, starting from lesson 82 and going to lesson 83. Once you get to line four of lesson 83 repeat the whole sequence. Do this a few times.

CHECK OUT VIDEO 23

1.

	High-E String (1st String)
	B String (2nd String)
	G String (3rd String)
0 2 3 2	D String (4th String)
2 2	A String (5th String)
3	Low-E String (6th String)

2.

	High-E String (1st String)
0 1 0	B String (2nd String)
2 2	G String (3rd String)
0 4 4	D String (4th String)
	A String (5th String)
	Low-E String (6th String)

3.

	High-E String (1st String)
	B String (2nd String)
0 2 3 2	G String (3rd String)
2 2	D String (4th String)
3	A String (5th String)
	Low-E String (6th String)

4.

	High-E String (1st String)
	B String (2nd String)
	G String (3rd String)
0 2 3 2	D String (4th String)
2 2	A String (5th String)
3 3	Low-E String (6th String)

Lesson 84: Licks Inspired by Great Rock Guitarists: Pete Townshend & The Edge

Here are two exercises to embellish your chord playing. They are based on ideas that you can find in music by U2 and The Who. Both The Edge (from U2) and Pete Townshend (from The Who) use suspensions in their rhythm guitar playing to add color to the chords. Suspensions are notes added just above or below a note of a chord. The suspension temporarily replaces one of the chord's notes. This creates a little bit of tension, which is then resolved once the suspended note is replaced by a chord tone. The most common suspensions replace the third of a chord.

**CHECK OUT
VIDEO 24**

The Edge and Pete Townshend are both extraordinary guitarists and songwriters. Their styles, though not outwardly flashy, are highly expressive and unique. Often, instead of blasting the listener with flurries of scorching notes (although nothing is wrong with that), they devise intricate and subtle sonic atmospheres that create worlds for each song that they play.

These two licks use suspended chords. Lick one can be used in conjunction with a D Major chord. Lick two can be used to embellish an A Major chord. Try playing each lick alone; then play them one after the other. Once you have the idea down, you might also try arpeggiating the sequences. Have Fun!

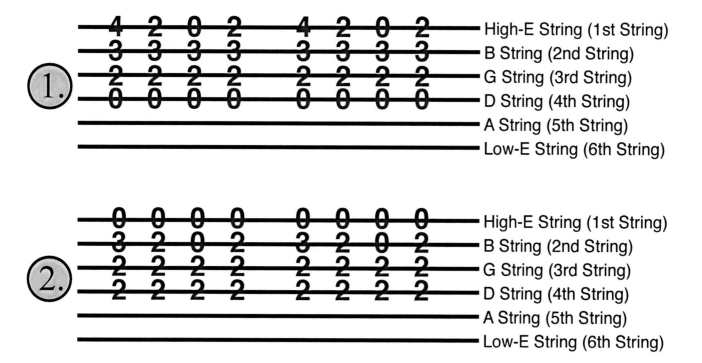

Lesson 85: Check Out These Songs for Rhythm Guitar

Take a little time now and listen to the following rock songs that use rhythm guitar techniques and chords. You might check out YouTube or the artists' websites for free recordings and performance videos. Listen to the guitar parts in each song and try to pick up ideas and sounds for licks and chords, which you can then add to your own playing. Take a moment and listen to these songs in an active way, focusing on the guitar sound for each artist.

Here are a few:

- The Who: *Pinball Wizard*

- Eric Clapton: *Layla (Unplugged Version)*

- U2: *Where the Streets Have No Name*

- Jimi Hendrix: *The Wind Cries Mary*

- The Rolling Stones: *Jumpin' Jack Flash*

- The Stray Cats: *Rock This Town*

- Dire Straits: *Sultans of Swing*

- Eric Johnson: *Forty-Mile Town*

- Led Zeppelin: *Over the Hills and Far Away*

Lesson 86: Chapter 3 Overview
What We Have Learned

Take a little time to go back over some of the concepts from this chapter's lessons. If there was an element that you were not sure about spend a day or two and go back over the lesson. If there is a corresponding video, check that out as well.

- Rhythm Guitar Basics

- Strumming Patterns

- Palm Muting

- Funk Style

- Reggae Style

- Trying Out New Gear

- Major Barre Chords

- Minor Barre Chords

- Dominant Seventh Barre Chords

- Arpeggiating Chords

- Bass Lines

- Suspensions

- Music Theory: Notes of the Second String

- Licks Inspired by The Edge and Pete Townshend

- Songs That Use Rhythm Guitar Techniques

CHAPTER FIVE: LEAD GUITAR BASICS

Lesson 87: Lead Guitar Overview

In this chapter, we are going to look at some beginning concepts in lead guitar playing. Each of these lessons is the starting point for you to explore broader concepts and to develop your own style (remember, learning guitar is a lifelong journey). Good lead guitar playing is a vital and important part of Rock music. It not only helps build the energy and intensity of the music, but, along with rhythm guitar playing, it helps to tell the story of a song by creating meaningfully related melodies and licks.

The lead guitar techniques that are covered here will definitely spice up your playing. These techniques may take a little while to master; so, be patient. The first few lessons go over hammer-on and pull-off techniques. These are cool sounding techniques where you will create expressive notes on your guitar without plucking the note. Next, we have a brief overview of guitar pedals. These are box-shaped devices, linked to your guitar and amp by cables. Pedals are designed to change--both drastically and subtly--the sound of your guitar. They can add distortion, make the notes echo, sound like it is underwater, really, in a way, "the sky is the limit". There is a video that coincides with the lesson to give you an idea of the sounds that pedals create. Near the end of the chapter, we will go over string bending and double stops. String bending is a technique where you raise the pitch of a note by bending the string up or down. This technique will bring us into Advanced-Beginner Rock guitar territory; it requires a little bit of finger strength and control. So, take your time with this technique. Double Stops are another technique that we will add to our lead-guitar bag of tricks. These are licks that you can use to add a high-energy Blues feel to your playing. At the end of the chapter, there is a big, four-line lick that encompasses many of the techniques that we have learned.

There are hundreds (more likely thousands) of great lead guitarists in Rock. Over the next few years, you should take a little time each week to discover new ones. Here are just a few (of the many) great Rock guitarists whose lead guitar playing you should check out to get some inspiration for your own playing: Eddie Van Halen, Jimi Hendrix, Dickey Betts, Eric Johnson, John Frusciante, Richie Blackmore, Steve Morse, Kurt Cobain, Joe Perry, Jack White, Jeff Beck, The Edge, Brian May, Mark Knoplfer, Tom Morello, Ry Cooder, Carlos Santana, Jerry Garcia, Kirk Hammett, Jimmy Page, Stevie Ray Vaughan, Chuck Berry, Eric Clapton, Duane Allman, Joe Satriani, Steve Vai, Steve Howe, Greg Howe, John-5, David Gilmour, and Alex Lifeson.

Lesson 88: Rock Technique
Pull Offs & Hammer Ons

CHECK OUT VIDEO 25

In the next few lessons, we are going to look at hammer-on and pull-off techniques on the guitar. These are two techniques that will add some new sound colors to your guitar pallet. Used by countless lead guitarists, they are often employed in conjunction with each other. Both techniques require a little time to master; so, it is only natural that it may take a week or two to get them under your belt. Take your time and have fun!

PULL OFFS

Pull offs are a guitar technique where you fret a note and pull your finger down and off of the string without plucking the second note. You can pull off to another fretted note, for example, from the third finger to the first finger, or you can pull off from a fretted note to an open string. The technique should probably be called "pull downs", because that is a closer description of the motion. It is important that you use the tip of your finger when doing a pull off. This will give a more precise tone and make the technique easier to execute. Check out the video.

HAMMER ONS

Hammer ons are almost the opposite of pull offs. They are a technique where you bring a finger in your left hand down quickly on a fret without plucking the string with your right hand. This technique can be done with any finger of the left hand; however, it is easiest to execute with the index finger. For hammer ons, it is very important to use the tip of your left-hand finger as the striking surface on the string. This will ensure that the sound is very resonant and well formed. Also, to create effective hammer ons, it is more important use speed, rather than power with the motion of your left-hand finger. It should come down on a fret with a fast, but not too powerful, hammer-like motion. The corresponding video on hammer ons will give you a better idea about how to play them and how they sound. This is a case where it is easier to understand a concept in an audio / visual presentation, rather than just reading about it in a book format.

Lesson 89: Rock Technique Pull-Off Licks

Here are four guitar licks that use pull-off techniques and open strings. Try them one at a time, starting slowly and gradually increasing the speed. Remember to use the tips of your fingers.

CHECK OUT VIDEO 26

1.

```
3 2 0 3 2 0 3 2 0 3 2 0 ── High-E String (1st String)
─────────────────────────── B String (2nd String)
─────────────────────────── G String (3rd String)
─────────────────────────── D String (4th String)
─────────────────────────── A String (5th String)
─────────────────────────── Low-E String (6th String)
```

2.

```
─────────────────────────── High-E String (1st String)
3 2 0          3 2 0        ── B String (2nd String)
3 2 0      3 2 0         0 ── G String (3rd String)
        3 2 0      3 2 0 ── D String (4th String)
─────────────────────────── A String (5th String)
─────────────────────────── Low-E String (6th String)
```

3.

```
3 2 0 5 3 0 7 5 0 5 3 0 ── High-E String (1st String)
─────────────────────────── B String (2nd String)
─────────────────────────── G String (3rd String)
─────────────────────────── D String (4th String)
─────────────────────────── A String (5th String)
                         0 ── Low-E String (6th String)
```

4.

```
─────────────────────────── High-E String (1st String)
1 0 3 0 5 0 6 0 8 ── B String (2nd String)
─────────────────────────── G String (3rd String)
─────────────────────────── D String (4th String)
─────────────────────────── A String (5th String)
─────────────────────────── Low-E String (6th String)
```

Lesson 90: Rock Technique Hammer-On Licks

Here are four guitar licks that use hammer-on techniques and open strings. Try them one at a time, starting slowly and gradually increasing the speed. Remember to use the tips of your fingers.

CHECK OUT
VIDEO 26

1.

	High-E String (1st String)
	B String (2nd String)
0 0 0	G String (3rd String)
0 2 0 2 0 2	D String (4th String)
	A String (5th String)
	Low-E String (6th String)

2.

	High-E String (1st String)
	B String (2nd String)
	G String (3rd String)
0 0 0	D String (4th String)
0 3 0 3 0 3	A String (5th String)
	Low-E String (6th String)

3.

0 2 3 0 3 5 0 5 7 0 3 5	High-E String (1st String)
	B String (2nd String)
	G String (3rd String)
	D String (4th String)
	A String (5th String)
0	Low-E String (6th String)

4.

	High-E String (1st String)
	B String (2nd String)
0 0 0	G String (3rd String)
3 5 3 5 3 5	D String (4th String)
	A String (5th String)
	Low-E String (6th String)

Lesson 91: Guitar Pedals

Guitar pedals (or "stomp boxes") are electronic devices, usually in the shape of a metal or plastic box, which are placed on the floor and connected between an electric guitar and amp by cables. Pedals can change a guitar tone subtly or dramatically, depending on the model and specific effect. Pedals can create echoes, distortion, underwater sounds, and many other tones. In general, they are controlled by an on-off switch that the guitarist taps with his or her foot.

CHECK OUT VIDEO 27

To the Left are various guitar pedals

Distortion Pedals: These effect pedals simulate the distortion created by vacuum tubes, transistors, or digital circuits in guitar amps. When overdriven, these amps produce a type of distortion that is musically pleasing. These pedals create this well-known Rock sound.

Reverb: These effects simulate the sound of acoustic environments such as rooms, concert halls, caverns, or an open space. You can really shape your sound with reverb.

Chorus Pedals: These effects enrich the incoming signal and create the impression that multiple instruments or voices are being played in unison. The slight delay time that the pedal creates simulates the subtle pitch and timing differences heard when several musicians or vocalists perform together.

Delay Pedals: These effects repeat your guitar signal after a given time period, creating an echo effect. Each subsequent repeat is a little quieter than the previous one.

Check out the video for a more in-depth explanation with examples.

Lesson 92: Rock Technique Double Stops

Double stops are a great and relatively easy guitar technique that you can use to spice up your playing. They can be used to energize your lead playing or give some extra power to your rhythm work.

CHECK OUT VIDEO 28

The idea for a double stop is that you will play two strings at the same time (usually adjacent strings). Most of the time, you can just use the flat part / pad of your index finger (where your finger print is located) and place it over two adjacent strings.

This effect will give a fuller sound to your playing. Try placing your index finger over the 3rd fret of the 1st and 2nd strings (the High-E string and the B string) and strum those strings together. You will hear the sound of a perfect 4th interval (the notes "D" and "G") as the strings ring together. This is a "classic" Rock guitar sound and can be heard on thousands of recordings.

Now, try placing your index finger over the 3rd fret of the 1st and 2nd strings (the High-E string and the B string) and strum those strings together three times. Then, move your index finger up to the 5th fret on the 1st and 2nd strings and strum those strings three times. Listen to the sound quality. See example 1 below.

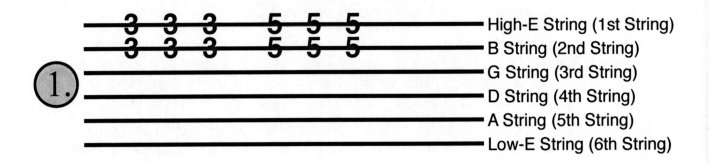

```
  ---3---3---3-------5---5---5------- High-E String (1st String)
  ---3---3---3-------5---5---5------- B String (2nd String)
1.---------------------------------- G String (3rd String)
  ---------------------------------- D String (4th String)
  ---------------------------------- A String (5th String)
  ---------------------------------- Low-E String (6th String)
```

Double stops are used in songs by Aerosmith, The Rolling Stones, Eric Johnson, Stevie Ray Vaughan, Chuck Berry, Eric Clapton, ACDC, The Doors, and Van Halen.

Lesson 93: Rock Technique Double-Stop Licks

Here are four guitar licks that use double-stop techniques. Try them one at a time, starting slowly and gradually increasing the speed. Remember to use the tips of your fingers.

CHECK OUT VIDEO 29

1.

High-E String (1st String)
B String (2nd String)
3 2 0 3 2 0 3 2 0 — G String (3rd String)
3 2 0 3 2 0 3 2 0 — D String (4th String)
A String (5th String)
Low-E String (6th String)

2.

High-E String (1st String)
B String (2nd String)
5 3 0 5 3 0 5 3 0 — G String (3rd String)
5 3 0 5 3 0 5 3 0 — D String (4th String)
A String (5th String)
Low-E String (6th String)

3.

1 3 3 3   6 3 3 3 — High-E String (1st String)
1 3 3 3   6 3 3 3 — B String (2nd String)
G String (3rd String)
D String (4th String)
A String (5th String)
0 — Low-E String (6th String)

4.

6 3 3 3   1 3 3 3 — High-E String (1st String)
6 3 3 3   1 3 3 3 — B String (2nd String)
G String (3rd String)
D String (4th String)
A String (5th String)
Low-E String (6th String)

Lesson 94: Rock Technique String Bending

Bending the strings is a great technique to add expressiveness to your lead guitar playing. Basically, you will push the string up far enough to get the pitch to change (to go higher). This takes a good deal of effort. So, the key is to use three of your fingers to bend the string, instead of just the finger on the fret you're trying to bend. You can accomplish this by placing your third finger on the fret you're trying to bend. Place your first and second fingers on the frets behind it, and exert power with all three fingers pushing upward and down on the string. It's easiest to bend notes on the 2nd string. Make sure you check out the video to see the technique in action.

CHECK OUT VIDEO 30

On the second string, place your index finger on the 6th fret, middle finger on the 7th fret, and ring finger on the 8th fret. Use the strength of all three fingers together to bend (push) the note on the eighth fret up a half step.

Half

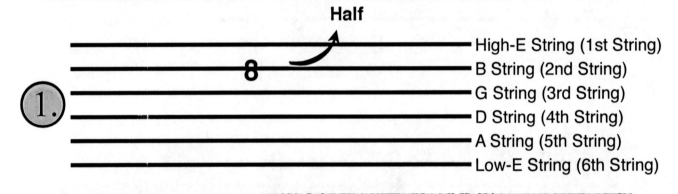

1.

- High-E String (1st String)
- B String (2nd String)
- G String (3rd String)
- D String (4th String)
- A String (5th String)
- Low-E String (6th String)

On the second string, place your index finger on the 6th fret, middle finger on the 7th fret, and ring finger on the 8th fret. Use the strength of all three fingers together to bend (push) the note on the eighth fret up a whole step.

Full

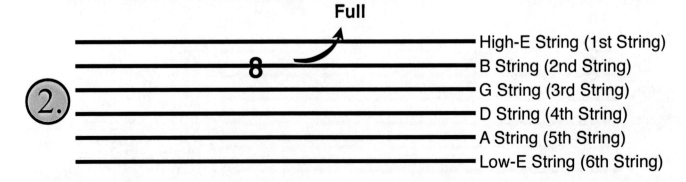

2.

- High-E String (1st String)
- B String (2nd String)
- G String (3rd String)
- D String (4th String)
- A String (5th String)
- Low-E String (6th String)

Lesson 95: Rock Technique String Bending Licks

Here are four guitar licks that use string bending. Try them one at a time, starting slowly and gradually increasing the speed. The string bends are for a whole step and are marked "Full".

CHECK OUT VIDEO 31

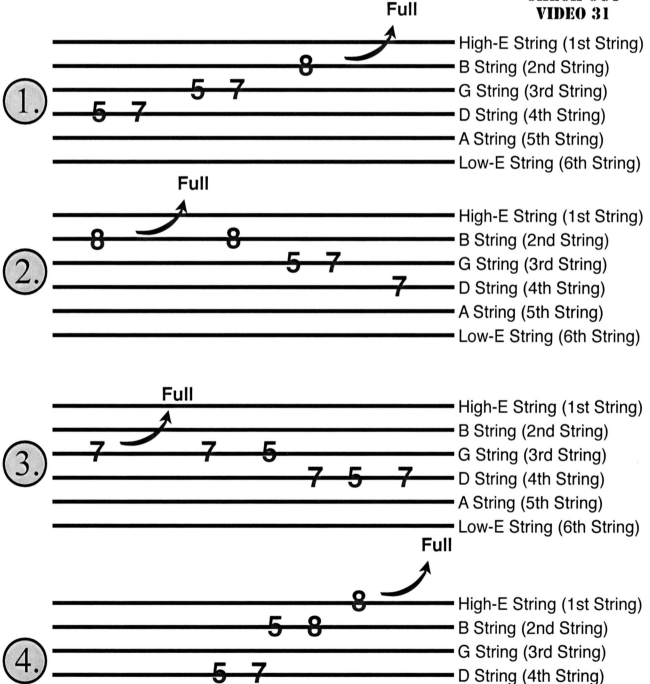

Lesson 96: Secret to Guitar Success #10: Have Confidence in Your Musicality

One of the most important aspects to your sound and musicality is confidence. Without it your playing will be anemic and bloodless. So, even from the beginning of your journey with the guitar, cultivate an attitude of assurance and grace. Your confidence does not need to be loud and brash (although that is fine, if that's your musical personality); it can also be solid and quietly strong.

One of the best ways to build your confidence with the guitar is to get out and play with people. Little by little, you and your friends may form a band and play gigs around your town. The more that you do this, the easier it will be to get up in front of of a crowd. For most guitarists, performing is a skill that needs to be developed (just like learning chords, licks, and scales). So, the step now would be to learn some songs, start playing them with friends, and, then, set up some gigs (most likely for free) at your school, local coffee shop, religious institution, etc. This is what it is all about after all.

Lesson 97: Secret to Guitar Success #11: Develop Your Own Musical Voice

In the end, wherever your guitar playing takes you, the most vital aspect of your musicality is the development of your own artist voice. This is an ongoing, lifelong process and it is composed of many elements ranging from your musical influences, the books you have read, your favorite foods, your life experiences (from the monumental to the seemingly trivial), and the musicians with whom you create music. Over time, your musical voice will evolve, based on all of these influences and perceptions. You should be open to these developments, because having music in your life--however big or small--gives it a sense of adventure.

This book and video course is only a starting point for your Rock guitar playing. I hope that it has been helpful in giving you insights and solid foundation into techniques, licks, and some basic music theory used in Rock styles. All of the licks and techniques presented should serve as springboards to your own playing and the development of your musical voice; so, feel free to explore each one and create variations based on your own expression. Of all of these "secrets" to guitar success, the first and last (numbers one and eleven) are the most important: Cultivate a positive attitude in your music making and develop your musical voice.

Lesson 98: Crafting Good Guitar Solos

Creating a guitar solo is like composing some music on the spot. Great guitarists seem to be in the moment as they improvise. Even though they have some licks and stylistic flourishes that they play, they also bring in something that is new and vibrant.

When you create your guitar solos you might also consider to act, in a way like a musical storyteller. For your solo, you might try to make a beginning, middle and end. At the beginning of your solo, you might take some notes or phrases from the melody of the song. The audience's ears will pick up on this and be curious. Then, start to add some notes or rhythms that are not part of the melody. As you do this, you might also add a little tension by moving to higher notes on the guitar. By using some of the techniques that you have learned from this book, like bends, hammer ons and pull offs, slides, and vibrato, you can add interest and variety to your solo. Then, you should strive to reach the pinnacle note of your solo. This does not need to be the highest note of your solo; however, it should probably be a note related to the main chords (most likely the root note) of the song. Then, as an ending, you might create a little outro: a kind of closing statement where the guitar fades back into the texture of the song.

This story-telling approach to guitar solos is a good first step, and, as most techniques in this book it is a starting point for you to explore musical ideas. One thing that you might consider with this approach is the emotional trajectory of your solo. For example, you might start things out quietly with some slow, repeated notes and then build up to some fiery high notes and string bends. Another approach would be to start things out with a roar and some wild playing and then gradually simmer things down or make a transition to a happier range of expression. The choice is yours here. That's what makes things fun and interesting. Do your best to explore your creativity and your own musical voice.

Guitar Solos That Have a Storytelling Approach:

Hotel California: Don Felder & Joe Walsh, guitarists

Desert Rose: Eric Johnson, guitarist

All Along the Watchtower: Jimi Hendrix, guitarist

Comfortably Numb: David Gilmour, guitarist

Stairway to Heaven: Jimmy Page, guitarist

Layla: Eric Clapton and Duane Allman, guitarists

Texas Flood: Stevie Ray Vaughan, guitarist

Surfing with the Alien: Joe Satriani, guitarist

Lesson 99: Getting Different Tones from Your Guitar

THE ANGLE AND PLACEMENT OF THE PICK

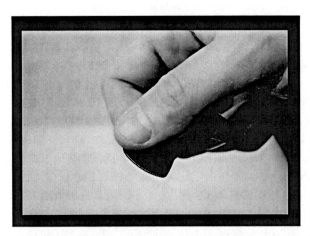

By changing the angle, speed, and power of your picking motion in the right hand, you can greatly vary the tone of your guitar playing. The guitar pick is the point at which you come into contact with the strings. So, slight variations in the motion and angle will alter the guitar tone considerably. For most great players, the picking motion is the key to their sound.

Stevie Ray Vaughan, for example, had a very strong picking technique, where he attacked the strings with an aggressive motion. Eric Johnson, although he varies the angle frequently for different sounds, often uses a bouncing motion when picking to create an articulate, punching and round tone. In your own playing try moving the pick to different locations on the strings and plucking with the back of the pick or different sides. You will notice a great change in the tone quality. Also, put the pick down sometimes and just use your fingers.

TONE AND VOLUME CONTROLS

Another great way to vary the tone of your guitar is to change the settings on the volume and tone knobs on your guitar.

If you are playing with distortion and a lead tone, try turning the volume knob down a few settings. For instance, try turning it from ten down to seven. You will hear the tone change and the sound will become a little cleaner.

The volume knob can also create volume-swell effects. Try this technique: turn the volume knob to zero, then strum a chord loudly and quickly turn the volume knob all the way up to ten. You will hear the sound fade in quickly. Try experimenting with the speed of the fade in. The tone knob can create wah-wah effects, in a similar way, when you pluck a note and turn the knob quickly from zero to ten.

Lesson 100: Grand Finale Lick!

Here is a "Grand-Finale" lick that uses a number of techniques that we have learned in the book and videos. The first line uses pull offs, the second line uses hammer ons, the third lines uses double stops and the fourth line uses the blues scale in G. *Have Fun!*

CHECK OUT VIDEO 32

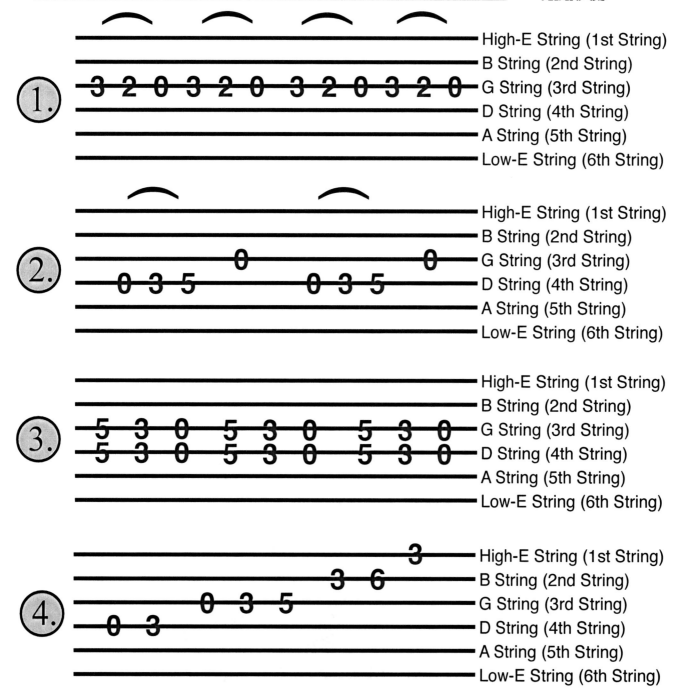

Congratulations!
Where to Go from Here

Great work in completing this book and video course on beginner Rock guitar. You are now developing an understanding of the fundamentals of Rock technique for guitar: major and minor chords, string bending, double stops, hammer ons, pull offs, slides, the Blues scale, power chords, basic music theory, the notes on the guitar neck, picking techniques, and strumming patterns. You are now able to apply this musical knowledge of the guitar to the songs that you play and write.

You can sign up for free guitar lessons in your inbox at www.steeplechasemusic.com.

Keep up the good work and continue to practice the guitar!

Damon Ferrante

Damon Ferrante is a Simkins Award-winning composer, guitarist, and music professor. When he was 8 years old, his uncle left an old electric guitar, which was in two pieces (neck and body separated) at his parents' house. Damon put the guitar together using some old screws and duct tape. That was the beginning of a wild ride through Rock, Jazz, Classical Music, and Opera that has spanned over 20 years.

Along the way, Ferrante has had performances at Carnegie Hall, Symphony Space, and throughout the US and Europe. He has taught on the music faculties of Seton Hall University and Montclair State University. He is the director of Steeplechase Arts & Productions, a company that he founded in 2003. You can catch him on tour throughout North America, Europe and Asia.

For more information about his books, check out:
www.SteeplechaseMusic.com.

This book is dedicated to my two uncles, Vincent and Jimmy. Each one played an important role in getting me started with Rock guitar, so many years ago. One gave me my first electric guitar: a red Harmony. The other shared records from his great Classic-Rock collection with me. Thank you both so much!

Appendix 1, Part 1

Chart 1:
Notes on the 5th & 6th Strings

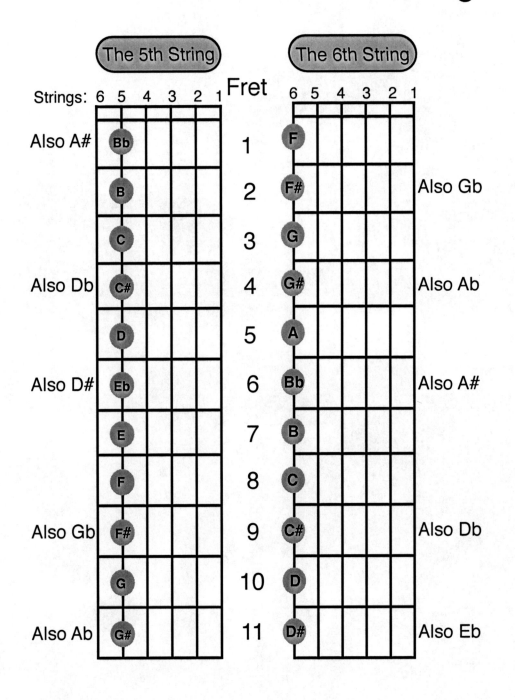

Appendix 1, Part 2

Chart 2:
Notes on the 4th & 3rd Strings

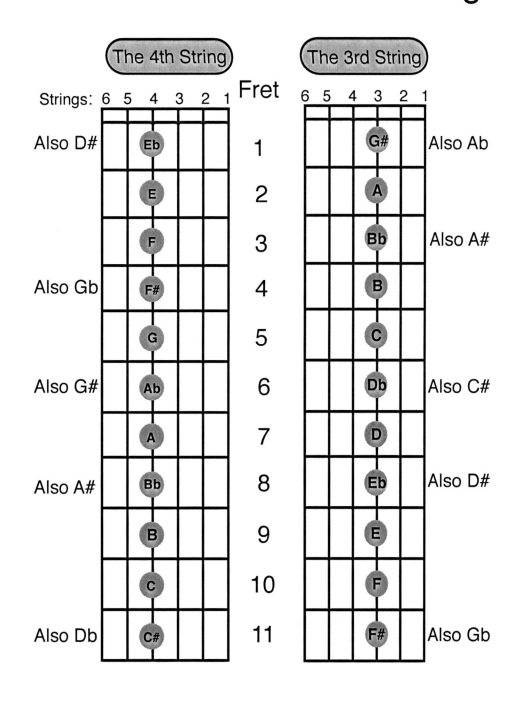

Appendix 1, Part 3

Chart 3:
Notes on the 2nd & 1st Strings

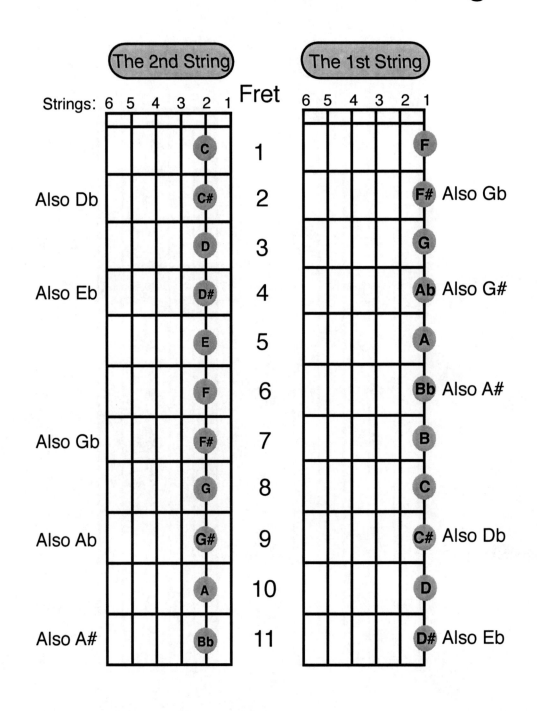

Master Guitar Technique!

Ultimate Guitar
Chords, Scales, & Arpeggios
Handbook

By Damon Ferrante
240 Lessons For All Levels:
Book & Video Course

Master Piano Technique!

Piano Scales Chords
Arpeggios Lessons

Book & Videos   Damon Ferrante

CPSIA information can be obtained
at www.ICGtesting.com
Printed in the USA
LVOW09s1959200217
524838LV00015B/497/P